The Secret to the Christian Life—

Have We Overlooked
the Main Point?

Books by Gene Edwards

In a Class by Itself
The Divine Romance

Introduction to the Deeper Christian Life
Living by the Highest Life
The Secret to the Christian Life
The Inward Journey

Books on Inner Healing
A Tale of Three Kings
The Prisoner in the Third Cell
Letters to a Devastated Christian
Climb the Highest Mountain
Exquisite Agony
Dear Lillian

Radical Books for Radical Christians
Overlooked Christianity
Rethinking Elders
Revolution: The Story of the Early Church
How to Meet in Homes
Beyond Radical

The First-Century Diaries
The Silas Diary
The Titus Diary
The Timothy Diary
The Priscilla Diary
The Gaius Diary

The Chronicles of Heaven
Christ Before Creation
The Beginning
The Escape
The Birth
The Triumph
The Return

THE

Secret

TO THE

Christian

Life

Acknowledgment

To Larry and Gretchen Hartzog, for allowing me the use of their beautiful summer home during the winter months, for it was there in the solitude of that lovely place this book found its beginning.

To Joe Punzalan, who has helped me with so many books by means of his shorthand and typing skills.

To Denise Sirois and Kathy Fuller, who labored so diligently on drafts two through twenty!

The Secret to the Christian Life
copyrighted by Gene Edwards
Printed in the United States of America
All rights reserved

Published by SeedSowers Publishing
P.O. Box 3317
Jacksonville, FL 32206
800.228.2665
www.seedsowers.com

Library of Congress Cataloging-in-Data
  Gene Edwards
  The Secret to the Christian Life / Gene Edwards
  ISBN 0-940232-74-X
  1. Christian Life

Times New Roman 12pt.

In Memoriam

He had been a missionary to Yugoslavia for many years, but I met him as my professor of church history at the Baptist Seminary in Ruschlikon, Switzerland, my first year in seminary. He laid a foundation in my life for a love of church history. His wife was friend and counselor to all of us who were students at the seminary. For her encouragement to me, I am forever her debtor. This book, then, is dedicated to two of the Lord Jesus' dear servants and to two lifelong friends.

Dr. John Allen Moore
Mrs. Pauline Moore

I neglect God
for the noise of a fly,
the rattling of a coach,
the creaking of a door.

John Donne

Contents

Preface

Somewhere among the piles of paper in my study is a list of books I hope to write before I die. At last count there were thirty-four! Of those, I count five as the most important of all. This book is one of those.

Be prepared, as you read this book, to see it cut across just about every concept you have on *how to live the Christian life*. I trust you will be able to adapt to such a different outlook. To my knowledge, there has never been a book written from this particular viewpoint. You may find a few paragraphs in a book or two that refer to the Christian life from this view, but never a book, nor even a chapter.*

One other observation. This marks only the second time I have penned a very personal book. That is, the word *I* appears fairly frequently. I trust you will find this an aid in the readability of the book, as that was my intent.

Now, may God bless your reading, and may he use this time to bring you further into him.

---

* If you are aware of such a book published previously to this one, I would like very much to know of it and will list it in this book in future editions.

Introduction

A large part of my last twenty-five years has been spent speaking to Christians who gather in homes (that is, to people who know *church* to be a living room full of believers). I have also spent a great deal of that time conducting conferences on *the deeper Christian life*. As a result of these two ministries, I have had the privilege of meeting some of the finest Christians of our age. By "finest" I mean folks who have a burning heart to know Christ better and are willing to admit their spiritual inadequacies in their walk with Christ. I minister to seekers, to the poor in spirit.

Sitting in these deeper Christian life audiences are laymen, pastors, ex-pastors, evangelists, missionaries, and other assortments of ministers and ex-ministers, all hungry people who, of course, are very familiar with the usual approach to "how to be a good Christian." Most of these Christians will tell you, "I've been through it *all.*" Many have been leaders or helpers in every interdenominational and nondenominational movement known to the English-speaking world. Some have belonged to really wonderful movements, others to some of the worst movements of the last hundred years. Every denomination imaginable has been represented, as well as just about every well-known conservative or fundamental seminary in the land. But all have one thing in common. Everyone has been taught some kind of "secret to the Christian life." And whatever this "secret" was, it was not working in their lives. Yes, there are other Christians for whom formulas work! But not for these folks.

My point? If the Christian life works for you, and if the "secret" you were taught is working for you, then you do not need this book. If what you have been given works, then fall down on your knees and thank God. You belong to a vast number of Christians. Stay with what works. But if you have tried all the "secrets" to the victorious Christian life and none of them have worked for you, this book may mark the beginning of a new adventure for you.

PART I

*Our love for Christ is tested
by whether we seek him, or
his gifts.*

ONE

Formulas Found Wanting

What have you been told is the secret to the Christian life? I have asked that question of thousands of Christians all across the English-speaking world, in traditional churches, in home churches, and in conferences. "What were you told you were supposed to do to be a good Christian? What were you taught about the secret to the Christian life?"

Do you recognize the answers I have received? They are presented to new Christians as standard issue. In fact, they are standard issue to *all* Christians. I present them here more or less in descending order:

- Pray and read your Bible
- Go to church

- Witness
- (Speak in tongues?)
- Tithe

Do these sound familiar? They are the most frequently heard. But here are more!

- Serve the Lord
- Go to Sunday school
- Learn positional truth
- Learn the exchanged life
- Go to a Christian college
- Go to a Bible school
- Go to a seminary
- Learn the faith-walk life
- Learn the faith-rest life

There are yet more: spiritual warfare, submission and authority, miracles, powers, obeying prophecy, reclaiming the gifts, head covering, peculiar dress, strict morals, (even) vegetarianism, becoming a covenant people, and the ever-familiar "Join our group because we are *it.*"

If those last ones seem a little out in left field, please know that there are a lot of other things growing out there in left field! Take a fresh look at what is taught by some of the most respected movements in Christendom, the denominations! They can scare the daylights out of you with their "secret to the Christian life." Often they will tell you that you absolutely must believe a certain doctrine because this doctrine is "essential." Other denominations will tell you there is but one way the Lord is going to come back to earth, "and you had better believe it, brother."

Or (we get the distinct feeling) it may be that when he comes you will get left behind because you did not believe he would come *in that particular way*. And so it goes.

Of course, I must not forget Southern Baptists (I am one). I can still hear preachers scaring the socks off of us, thundering about all sorts of plagues that might befall us if we did not "move our letter"!

Anyway, if any one of these "secrets" works for you, stick with it. *None* of them work for me. And for most of those to whom I minister, none work for them either.

In homes, over lunch, on the telephone, in letters by the boxful, and in conferences I have listened to seemingly endless numbers of believers recount how they have "tried everything and *none* of it works." Many tell their story with copious tears and speak from a broken heart. Christians of our era, as of every age for the last seventeen hundred years, are not and have not been equipped to answer the simple question:

> *How can I know Jesus Christ internally,*
> *personally, intimately, daily?*

Most of us could hasten to add: "And don't tell me to read my Bible and pray; I read my Bible more than you think, and I pray longer than you think. I want to know *Christ.*"

I cannot tell you the secret to the Christian life, but I can tell you this: For a large number of us, the previously mentioned lists do not work. For us, the answer lies somewhere else. What I will do in this book is introduce you to the possibility of a whole new vista from which to view the Christian life *and* practical ways to experience your Lord. But let me be quick to tell you, even this is not a cure-all for many of your Christian aches and pains. The aches and pains come with the Christian life.

Let me go on record. I do not believe anything on that list even comes close to the issue of how to live the Christian life. *All* have one inherent flaw.

The fatal flaw? Every item on the aforementioned list assumes that it is possible to live the Christian life. Can you live the Christian life? The answer is no, a resounding *no!* Don't faint. Read on! If that simple statement turns out to be true, then everything . . . absolutely everything . . . you have been taught concerning *the* "secret" will not work!

This book is written not so much to give you a cure-all as it is to move you completely away from the proposition that you *can* live the Christian life and to open up to you a whole new way to experience your Lord. Learn this simple, profound fact: You cannot live the Christian life. Learn that, and liberation is near.

This book is written to Christians who cannot live the Christian life. This book is for failures! (That, dear reader, is *all* of us . . . *including* a few folks out there who are masters of the bluff!)

That list you read a moment ago takes for granted you *can* live the Christian life. Also note that *you* are the center of every item on that list. *That* is the mountain you stand on today. Call it *you*-centeredness. *You* out there living the Christian life. We will move off of that mountain. In the pages that unfold, we will not only move off that mountain, we will go to a wholly different mountain, with a totally different vantage point. That is the purpose of this book, to get you off the mountain from which all those lists come and place you on the mountain you are supposed to be on . . . a mountain where . . . well, let's wait and see.

But there is one other purpose of this book. It will reveal to you *"the* secret to the Christian life" as it was known and experienced by *two* very important Ones! (In fact, you might say they were the first *two* Christians.) I make that statement without reservation or qualification!

As we turn from considering tithing and witnessing and going to church and being moral and, yes, even "Pray and read your Bible" as the secret to the Christian life, let us begin our search for something higher by asking a very simple question.

How did the *first* Christian live the Christian life? Can *he* teach us something we do not know? Does *he* know something we have overlooked? And that *second* Christian—of him we could ask the same question.

After that, we must ask an equally important question: "Have I been sentenced to live the Christian life by a means that is *different* from the way the very first Christian lived the Christian life?" That is, did the first Christian have an inside track, some way of living the Christian life that I do not have and *cannot* have? Are we second-class Christians who have to live the Christian life by a set of rules different from the first Christian?

You may not have recognized this, but you have been taught that very thing! It has been strongly implied that the very first Christian had an advantage over you. *He* lived the Christian life by one means, but you must live the Christian life by some other means. Your "how to" list and *his* "how to" list are different.

How do you feel about that? I will tell you how I feel. If it is really true that I have to live the Christian life differently from the way the first Christian lived it, I feel cheated!

So to begin our search, let us find that first Christian. When we do, we will ask him: "Did you live the Christian life by (1) going to church, (2) praying, (3) reading your Bible, (4) witnessing, (5) speaking in tongues, (6) tithing?" If that is how the first Christian lived the Christian life, then it follows that this is the way *you* must live the Christian life. But if that is not the secret to *his* daily walk, then that whole "how to" list you were taught is suspect. And if that turns out to be true, then this list is not for you either!

Here we go. Expect some major surprises. And expect a revolution!

TWO

Identifying the First
Visible Christian

Who was the first Christian?

Was Mary Magdalene the first Christian? She was the first to meet the resurrected Christ (John 20:10-18). Did she pray, read her Bible, go to church, witness, and tithe? I doubt it was that cut and dried with her. Or was Peter perhaps the first Christian? On the evening of the resurrection, the Lord Jesus awakened Peter's spirit and blew his divine nature into Peter (John 20:22)! Let's hope Peter was not the first Christian because he could not read. (There goes Bible study.)

And praying and tithing and going to church just do not seem to fit in here, either, do they?

But you and I both know that Peter and Mary Magdalene were not the first Christians. Who was? And how did he live the Christian life?

We know all things flow forth from the Godhead. Our answer lies in the fellowship of the Godhead; that is, in the fellowship of the Father, the Son, and the Spirit.

Once, two thousand years ago, the Eternal Son became incarnate. He "lived the Christian life" here on earth. As odd as it may seem to state the obvious, let us say that the Lord Jesus Christ was a Christian! Let us also say that he lived the Christian life. But let us *also* ask: "*How* did he live the Christian life?"

As you and I look at that question and explore its implications we may have to admit that our view of "how to live the Christian life" is going to have to undergo some serious changes! In fact, the usual way of viewing "how to live the Christian life" may have to be *dismantled.*

Let us look at Jesus Christ and his way of living the Christian life.

THREE

How Did Jesus Christ Live the Christian Life?

The Eternal Son came to earth and lived the Christian life . . . visibly. But pause for a moment. The Eternal Son is the *second* member of the Godhead (the Father, the Son, the Holy Spirit). Did it ever occur to you that your Lord . . . the Lord Jesus Christ . . . stated publicly that he could not live the Christian life? Of himself, he could not live the Christian life (John 5:30). Isn't that amazing! (So, if you're having a hard time, just consider John 5:30.) Now let us inquire of him, "How did *you* live the Christian life?"

Was the mainstay of his Christian life prayer and Bible study? He did pray, but was prayer the central pillar of his secret to living the Christian life?

That just does not seem to fit, does it? The Son of God depending on prayer and Bible study to make it through the day? Actually, this idea, your Lord *needing* to read his Bible every day to get through life as a believer, is an insult (1) to his preexistence in eternity and (2) to the fact that his Father indwelt him.

Your Lord did not live the Christian life by means of Bible study. But he quoted it, did he not? Does that not mean he was dependent on reading his Bible every day? And have we not often had pointed out to us his dependence on prayer and Bible study?

Your Lord is not so much the one who read the Scripture as he was the One who *wrote* it! *He is* the living Word. Back there in the age of the Old Testament, *he* spoke to men and *they* recorded *his* words.

Remember that day when Jesus Christ sat down in the synagogue in Nazareth and read the scroll of Isaiah. He also inaugurated his ministry that day. Well, he was *not* just quoting Isaiah; he was quoting Isaiah quoting this inaugural address to his earthly ministry! Isaiah quoted the Christ; the Christ did not quote Isaiah. As Jesus Christ sat in a Nazareth synagogue, he just may have been remembering the very hour, long ago, when he had spoken to Isaiah. As you read the four Gospels, you may want to note how often he *recalled* past events in history and past events in the heavenlies. For example, in John 17 he prayed, "Father, you loved me before the foundation of creation."

What of prayer? It is true that he rose early in the morning and went to a quiet place to pray. But do not read into such scenes the modern-day concept of what prayer is. Be careful, or you will see a man who is out there on his own all day long, praying, reading his Bible, and trying hard to be a good Christian . . . even a man so much on his own that he has to pray every morning without fail to make it through the day (making it through the day being dependent on his reading the Bible and praying *that morning*).

The fallacies of that scene are endless, but this one stands out the most. All day long the Lord Jesus was *not* alone. Your Lord was in *constant* contact with his Father. He was in constant *fellowship* with his Father. There was not one second when he was outside of constant, conscious fellowship with his Father. His Father spoke to him *constantly,* from within. His Father indwelt him. More incredibly, Jesus Christ did not speak unless he was aware of his Father's presence *and* his Father's internal speaking.

Jesus Christ had an indwelling Lord!

Never forget that your Lord was in constant *fellowship* with his Father.

Let us move on to another item on the list. Did tithing constitute some part in the Lord's "secret to living the Christian life?"

Did Jesus Christ tithe on a regular basis? We do not know. But if he did, that act did not constitute any part of his "secret" to the living of the Christian life.

Going to church?

A lot has been made of how Jesus faithfully attended the synagogue. People insist that since he went to synagogue, then some way that means *you* must go to church every Sunday morning at 11:00 A.M. Dear reader, how can reason get so farfetched? The ecclesia is not the synagogue. And, strictly speaking, you *can* "go to the synagogue," but you *cannot* "go to the church." No one ever thought of the idea of "going to church" until after A.D. 323. In the first Christian century the believers *were* the ecclesia.

The synagogue did not foreshadow the church. And Jesus Christ's living the Christian life was not dependent on the act of attending a synagogue meeting. God forbid!

I have a theory. When the Lord was a little boy, the idea of going to a dark, hot, stuffy, unventilated, smelly, windowless building to watch a long, drawnout, boring ritual in a language most of the people present could not understand was about as exciting to him as going to church and Sunday school was to you when you were ten years old. (How many tenyear-old boys have you ever met who were excited about going to church?)

Imagine your Lord, some Saturday in August, age ten, sitting in a synagogue, either on the floor or with his feet dangling from a bench. He sits there fighting to stay awake, waiting through two hours of misery, finally getting outside, gasping for air, and saying, "When I am grown, I'm going to start the ecclesia; and its meetings are going to be just like a synagogue service!"

In such a light, can you see the secret to the Christian life as lived by Jesus Christ being his study of the Bible, prayer, tithing, churchgoing, or a dozen other things you have been taught you must do "to be a good Christian"?

Then what was the Lord Jesus' *secret?* It began here: Jesus Christ found the Christian life as impossible to live as you and I do! Furthermore, he could not and did not live the Christian life. It is amazing, is it not, that Jesus publicly stated that fact, yet we have overlooked its significance.

Hold onto your traditions because there is more! I cannot live the Christian life. You cannot live the Christian life. Jesus Christ could not live the Christian life.

None of us can live the Christian life!

But here is something even more earthshaking. *Jesus Christ was not the first Christian!* We are looking in the wrong place for the first Christian. Someone else besides Jesus Christ was the *first* Christian.

Nor was Jesus Christ the person who "invented" the Christian life. The Christian life is older than A.D. 30, or even A.D. 1. The Christian life is *very* ancient. The Christian life is older than Moses, older than Abraham, older than Noah. The Christian life is even older than Adam! Yes, the Christian life was around long before man's creation! The Christian life, and the living of the Christian life, is older than space-time. The Christian life was here before eternity! Even more incredible, the Christian life is not native to this planet. Hear this: The Christian life is not native to *our* species. The Christian life is not native to our life form. It belongs exclusively to another life form! The Christian life was not, and is not, for human beings! The Christian life belongs to some other realm. Furthermore, the Christian life can be lived only by that *other* species.

Last of all, and most earthshaking, the Christian life can be lived only *in that other realm!* Repeat: The

Christian life can be lived only in the *spiritual* realm, in the spiritual creation. It cannot be lived in our physical creation, nor can the Christian life be lived by humans! The Christian life has never been lived *by* the physical, nor has the Christian life ever been lived *in* the physical realm. Now, if all these statements turn out to be true, it also follows that our species can never live the Christian life, and it follows that *you* cannot live the Christian life. And that fact will not be changed by your trying to do everything on that list in chapter 1.

Is this revolutionary enough for you? If not, read on.

Perhaps we have no greater need than to discover that there is only *one* Christian and there is only *one* person in all the universal creation who *can* live the Christian life, and that he lives the Christian life only in the realm of the spiritual. That one person who can live the Christian life is *not* the Lord Jesus Christ. Your Lord made it abundantly clear *he* could not live the Christian life, and that there was one, and only one, who could. Listen to the words of your Lord and Savior, the very Son of God.

> Without the Father,
> I can do *nothing.**

If Jesus Christ cannot live the Christian life, what makes you think that *you* can?

And all those people who told you that you could, where *did* they get such an idea? Can you succeed where your Lord could not? Dear reader, today can be

---

* See John 5:30, 8:28-29.

the greatest day you will ever live because today you can give up *trying* to live the Christian life! And if you do, you will be in good company because none of the rest of us can live the Christian life either. But there is one thing we all *can* do. We can all testify what a colossal failure we have been at trying to live the Christian life.

May I now have the privilege of introducing you to the first and *only* Christian . . . the *only* person who can live the Christian life. He is

God, the Father!

Father, I present to you another one of those poor, struggling souls trying to live the Christian life.

Dear reader, meet *the* secret to the Christian life, God the Father! Get to know this One, learn to relate to him . . . he is the only hope you will ever have for living the Christian life!

Now, by all means, let us ask the Father of our Lord Jesus Christ this question: "Father, how do *you* live the Christian life?"

And maybe we could even ask our Father: "Father, how did your Son, the Lord Jesus Christ . . . how did *he* live the Christian life on earth? And how did he live the Christian life back there in eternity past when he dwelt in you as the Eternal Son?"

FOUR

The Only Christian

The *only* Christian.*

If the Father does something, *that* is Christian. Whatever "Christian" is, that is the Father. *He* is Christian. Whatever the Father is not, *that* is not Christian. What he does is what a Christian does! What he is, is Christian. If he is, it is. If he is not, it is not. His very being is in itself . . . Christian. His thought, his action, his way *is* Christian. "Christian" is God the Father, and nothing else is. He himself is its definition.

Do you see that elderly gentleman over there? Yes, the distinguished white-headed gentleman in the

---

* Yes, you and I are Christians. But only *he* can live the Christian life. The *living* of the Christian life flows out to us . . . from him! We can be sure of one thing: *that* Christian knows how to live the Christian life. And he lives it!

rocking chair. The one who is piously reading his Bible. And praying! What a saintly sight he makes. In a minute, he is going to get up and go to church, and while there he is going to tithe. Is that God the Father? And is the Father's secret to the Christian life Bible study, prayer, going to church, and tithing? Well, first of all, that is very definitely not God the Father. That is my grandpa sitting over there in that rocking chair!*

But can you imagine superimposing such a scene on the Eternal God? Some folks do, it seems! The God of creation, reading his Bible, praying, and going to church in order to make it through the day being a good Christian! Why *not* superimpose that standard on God the Father? After all, that standard has been imposed on you.

Let us press this a little further. Can you see the Father of light having to fast or speak in tongues in order to live the victorious Christian life? Try to imagine that. It cannot be imagined. The mind refuses such an idea.

Then let us turn that picture around. Is it the God and Father of our Lord Jesus Christ who imposed this formula on *you?* Well, do you think God the Father imposed that standard, that method for Christian victory, *that* formula for living the Christian life . . . on his own Son? Did he tell his Son to read the Bible, pray, go to church, speak in tongues,

---

* My grandpa was a Louisiana Cajun who loved his Lord boundlessly. He was a total illiterate. But that did not stop Grandpa. He would ceremoniously pick up his Bible and hold it in front of him and stare at it intently for long periods of time. The problem was, he almost always held the Bible upside down! Now that is *really illiterate*; and, yep, that was *my* grandpa! And yes, he loved his Lord and spoke of his intimacy with the Lord in a way that few literate Bible scholars or Greek-reading theologians could ever hope to match!

and fast in order to be a good Christian? Do you think he did that?

Neither do I!

Let us seek to find some bedrock, some immovable principle of the Christian life. Where lies such a constant? We find immovable spiritual precepts in the God of eternity past. Go there to begin your search for the secret to the Christian life. Go to the Eternal God, in the eternals!

Let us do just that. Let us journey into eternity past. Forget formulas, forget neat schemes that have been made up by men stringing together a lot of verses taken out of context from all over the Bible and then dropping them on you, declaring with absolute certainty, "This is *the* way, now get to it!"

Let us visit the eternals *before* creation. There in the eternals, in the realm of the spirituals, let us ask God the Father, "How do you live the Christian life? What is *your* secret?" And in that same place let us ask, "How does the Eternal Son live the Christian life back here in the eternals?"

Before the incarnation, before creation, let us dare to inquire of the Eternal Son, "How did you live the Christian life back there in pre-eternity . . . long, long before you came to earth?"

Perhaps, in that primordial place, we will discover that truly we have overlooked the main point. Listen with all your heart, for you are about to discover the secret to the Christian life.

FIVE

The Christian Life in the Age before Eternity

The Christian life as lived out in the Godhead, before the eternals. Yes, even back then you find the Christian life . . . and it was being lived out in the Godhead. Here, at last, is bedrock! Here are the immovables. Here are the constants that never change. Whatever is going on *here,* you can be sure, foreshadows how *you* are to live the Christian life. Isn't that wonderful!

For a moment let's state the obvious, even though it may seem a little odd to do so: God the Father is a Christian . . . *and* he *lives* the Christian life! Also note: He is not a human; he is not of our species; he is not of our life form. Note further that the Christian life is being lived *only* by a higher form of life than human life, and the Christian life is being lived only by a spirit (God *is* spirit), and that such a life is being lived in the spiritual realm.

All of these elements made up the ingredients of the Christian life long before man came along. These elements are immovable! The Christian life was *not* being lived in the physical realm first! It was first lived in the eternals. And it was a way of living that belonged first to divinity, not humanity.

Now to our question, "How *does* God the Father live the Christian life?"

The answer is, he doesn't. He *is* the Christian life. He *is* the highest life, and only the highest life can live the Christian life. If you do not have the highest life, you cannot live the Christian life. If you have the highest life but do not live by that life, you cannot live the Christian life. *And* if you have *that* life but don't know it, well, you just may have a few problems finding the "start button" to the Christian life.

The Christian life is being lived in the spiritual realm. The Christian life belongs to the spiritual realm and can be lived only *in* the spiritual realm.*

The Christian life can be lived only by the divine species!

We have come, at last, to the ultimate wellspring, the original source, the taproot, the headwaters. *Here is our starting point.* Here we set out in quest of the secret to the Christian life. Begin anywhere else and you begin in the wrong place. And you will end up in the wrong place! God the Father is the wellspring, the source, the first motion, the fountainhead of the Christian life. He alone can live the Christian

---

* If this sentence is puzzling to you, just wait a few more pages.

life. His life form, and his life form alone, can live the Christian life.

Let us now, above all else, see this paramount truth. (Miss this and you will always mess up trying to live the Christian life.)

> 1. No one has ever lived the Christian life except God the Father. The Christian life is lived only by God the Father.

> 2. We live the Christian life only by means of the life of the Father. We live the Christian life by his life, the highest life. Divine life alone can live the Christian life.

You have never lived the Christian life except by means of the Father. That is, you have lived the Christian life only by his life, which dwells in you. And just where does his life dwell in you? His life dwells in your spirit. Not in your physical body, but in your very spiritual spirit! *He* lives the Christian life in you. He is a spirit, *the* spirit; he is a Christian, *the* Christian. He becomes factual, day-to-day, brass-tack reality, or the Christian life does not get lived!

Just try any other approach. Try! Then try *harder!* You still *cannot* live the Christian life! We need to pause here and consider that fact. Revelation alone causes you to realize that only your God can live the Christian life. It takes a revelation deep in your spirit to truly, truly know that *you* absolutely *cannot* live the Christian life.

How can you receive such a revelation? The answer to that is simple. Just keep on trying to live the Christian life. One day the revelation will hit you!

Try, and you *will* fail. This is not a platitude. This is stark reality—the way things really are.

We come now to the second immovable, but be careful to let the *first* of these immovables sink into you. Otherwise, you may end up seizing on only the second.

The second immovable fact about the Christian life is that *he* must live the Christian life *in* you. But be careful of that statement. There is a long, venerable (and very shallow) tradition among Christians to glibly go around saying, "We must let Christ live the Christian life through us." That is an often-uttered statement, and it is a very correct statement! But it is a statement that is nearly always made with utterly no experiential backing, and it virtually never comes with an instruction book.

I am amazed, even stunned, as to how totally void the Christian family is of understanding how to make this glorious fact *practical*. It seems to me our libraries should be filled with books giving practical help on this subject. Christian literature is almost void of practical direction given to the Christian about how Jesus Christ lives his life through us. Just how does it come about, *practically,* that Jesus Christ lives his life in you? How does *he* live the Christian life for you? Is it possible we never get told the answer because no one knows what to tell us? "Let Jesus Christ live the Christian life through you" is a great one-liner to repeat in a sermon or in a devotional, but it is a totally worthless statement unless one has grasped the depth of that *first* fact. *You cannot live the Christian life.* It remains worthless unless someone gives you some very practical handles.

It almost goes without saying that you must lay hold of that higher life that lives inside of you, for *that* life alone can live the Christian life. Puppy dogs cannot live the human life because only human beings can live the human life. Puppy dogs are the wrong life form for living the human life. Humans cannot live the Christian life because the Christian life is the exclusive territory of the *highest* life form.

How important is it that you understand that you *cannot* live the Christian life? Well, how important was it that Jesus Christ understood that *he* could not live the Christian life? He understood! You need to understand this every bit as much as he did!

If your Lord could not live the Christian life, then how is it that he is credited with having lived the Christian life? The answer is: (1) his Father lived inside him, and (2) his Father lived the Christian life in him. This could mean only one thing: Jesus Christ had laid hold of that higher life that was inside him (in his spirit); he had laid hold of this life of his Father's in a very living way. He *knew* an indwelling Lord very, very well.

The Father indwelt his Son here on this earth for thirty-three years. The *Father* lived the Christian life *inside* Jesus Christ. It was the Father's life, and the Father's life alone, that lived the Christian life inside your Lord. It is the Father's life, and the Father's life alone, that ever lives the Christian life. It is the Father's life, and the Father's life alone, that will live the Christian life in *you*. Set your course in any other direction, embrace a *formula* or a *list* in order to "live the Christian life," and you are doomed to frustration.

You cannot live the Christian life. But, oh dear reader, you can certainly *fail trying!*

Thank God for the failure, because it is that constant failure that causes us to drag our nearly lifeless bodies up to the Lord Jesus and say, "I give up, Lord! I cannot live the Christian life!" *That* will mark the most wonderful moment in your Christian life, and the hour the living of the Christian life really begins for you! It will be the day you give up trying. Either by revelation or by empirical experience, you will have discovered that you just are not one of those people who can live by all those formulas . . . and on that day you are a candidate for the Father's life being lived out in you.

Yes, it is true that as a believer you do have his life in you! But on the day you quit trying to live the Christian life . . . then you will *finally* give him the freeway to live out in you what is so easy and so simple and so organic for *him* to do!

Right now would be a good time for you to shed your efforts at trying to be a good Christian. This is a perfect place to lay down trying to live the Christian life. (You might as well, as you *are* going to fail at it anyway.) But if the Lord has not shown you this, oh, dear Christian, just you keep on trying. In fact, try even harder! One day you will come around and join the society of those of us who failed at being good Christians! How can I be so certain that you will join us one day? Because "fail" is the only thing a Christian trying to live the Christian life *can* do!

Hopefully, you just got set free from a long list of

dos and don'ts (the dos you can't do, and the don'ts you always do). Why look so shocked; stop and think about it. You never were any good at living the Christian life. Admit it. Deep down inside, you really did not like going to church; praying was always a burden; and there were lots of times all the pages in your Bible were blank, no matter where you turned. And if you cannot face up to those real, honest, truthful *facts,* you will never come to the end of your struggle and the beginning of really knowing him . . . of knowing the many-splendored glory of his living his own life in you!

We are standing before the Godhead in eternity past. We have visited an age that preceded creation. It is imperative that here, in this place, we now speak with the Eternal Son.

"Lord, how did you—living *in* the Eternal Father— how did you live the Christian life, in the eternals, before creation?"

Dear reader, whatever was the secret of the Eternal Son, believe it or not, that secret also belongs to you. His answer, his way of living the Christian life, is for you today!

Let us now find *his* answer!

SIX

"The Christian Life"
in the Godhead

With awe and with trembling, let us come to the very center of the being of the Godhead. There we behold the Father, the Son, and the Holy Spirit in fellowship with one another. (Don't bother looking for tongues, Bible, tithes, fasting, church buildings, or prayer.)

Reverently we ask the Son, "How do you, here in eternity past . . . by what means do you . . . live the Christian life?"

If you can see what is going on in the Godhead—if you can see how the Christian life is lived out, there in *that* place—then you can see the Christian life as it is to be lived out by *you*. Either that is true or there are *two ways* to live the Christian life, one way for God's Son and *another* way for you and me.

Behold the relationship of the Son to the Father. In

31

so doing you behold the first and most elemental principle of *how* you are to live the Christian life. Here is *his way.* The prime move, the first motion, is *here.* And what do we discover?

Here is the first thing we discover.

The Father gives his life to his Son. This is how it all begins. That is step one in the living out of the Christian life!

Out of sheer love and grace the Father imparts to his Son the very life by which the Father "lives the Christian life." The Father gives his Son his very own life so that his Son may also live by *that* life. The life the Father imparted to the Son is the life by which the Son lives. The Father bequeaths his life to his Son, and the Son lives by means of the Father.

This was the origin of the living out of the Christian life by someone other than the unbegotten Father. Here is the second member of the Godhead. This is how he lived before the Father.

The Father imparts to the Son the only life that can live the Christian life. The Son now lives by means of that life. So begins the chronicle of the Christian life. Later when this Eternal Son comes to earth as a carpenter, he will tell people his secret.

> The life I live
> I live by means
> of my Father.
> (John 6:57)

Before we go on, please note again that this is taking place in the realm of the spiritual, and that the Father's life is *spirit.* (Anatomically, God is spirit—not physical. His makeup is spirit.)

Now, what is the *next* stage these two experience together after the Father gives his life to the Son? Something beautiful! The Father, by means of his own divine life, turns to his Son and *loves* the Son. The Son, by means of his Father's life, *receives* the Father's love. Even the *receiving* of love is by means of the Father's life. Then the Son (again by means of his Father's life) returns that love to the Father.

The Father loves the Son; the Son loves the Father.

Life given, love exchanged. *That* is the Christian life before creation. We are now deep into the innermost secret of the Christian life: a giving of life, and an exchange of love.

Just look at the *simplicity* of the Christian life back then!

(1) The Father gives his life to his Son; all the Son will ever do, he will do by means of his Father's life. (2) Then the Father loves the Son. (3) And then the Son, by means of the Father's life, loves the Father back. These are the first elements of "living the Christian life" as they were first known and experienced and expressed.

So was it then. So is it now. *So shall it ever be!*

These simple elements are the most essential elements in all that is in any way related to living the Christian life. For whom? For all—including *you!*

Note, this is not head knowledge. This is not that "mindy" thing called positional truth. This is head-on, empirical, spiritual, practical, *experiential* experience!

We now move on, but the simplicity continues.

Next the Father *speaks* to the Son. The Son hears

and, having the Father's very own life in him, responds to what he hears from the Father.

The Father speaks to the Son; the Son hears and responds to the Father.

Life. Love. Speaking. Listening. How incredibly simple!

Now we come to the most central element of all.

Beholding.

The relationship of the Father and Son, whatever else it is, is centered in each *beholding* the other. The Father is ever before the face of the Son. The Son ever beholds the face of his Father. The center of their *fellowship* is *beholding.* See the Father beholding the Son.

Dear reader, there is no more central issue in your life, and there will never be, than that of *learning* to behold! *You* beholding the Father, and you beholding the Son. But is that possible for you? Yes! By means of his life in you, and by doing the beholding *in* that other realm! What realm is the "other" realm? The realm of the spirit.*

Life. Love. Speaking. Hearing. And now, beholding!

Simplicity itself!

The giving and receiving of life, the loving and being loved, the speaking and the hearing, and now the *beholding* . . . all are initiated by the Father. The engine of the Christian life, for the Son of God, is his

---

* We will not leave this point until you have been given practical equipment to aid you in beholding the Father and beholding the Son. You, joining into their fellowship, in your spirit!

Father! These are the constants, the immovables, of the Christian life.

You must consider these simple elements as being central to your Christian walk also. If the Son lives the Christian life, it is only by means of the Father's life imparted to him. There is no other means available for living the Christian life . . . for him or for you. Here, dear reader, is the direction for you to take in your quest of the living out of the Christian life.

See how truly ancient is the living out of the Christian life! The living of the Christian life belongs to another realm, to another species, and is the exclusive territory of the highest life form, God himself. And remember, the Christian life is lived *only* in the spiritual realm. Also, the Christian life was around long before prayer, before the New Testament, and surely before going to church on Sunday, fasting, tithing, or speaking in tongues!

Let us look a little closer at this relationship of the Father and the Son. Once again, the elements. The imparting of the highest life. The Son living by means of that life. The Father loving the Son. The Son loving the Father in return. The speaking. The responding. The Father beholding the Son. The Son ever beholding the Father. Do you see a principle at work here? The principle is *intra-exchange*.

There is an *exchange* going on within the Godhead. There is a pouring out of a spiritual experience of the Father, from the Father. The Son receives the Father's experience, experiences what the Father experienced, and then returns that experience back to the Father.

Life pours out from the Father and "radiates" that

life to the Son. The Son receives and experiences what the Father poured out upon the Son. The Son re-bounds that same life back to the Father. The Father loves the Son. The Son, *irradiated* by his Father's love, experiences that love, and now re-radiates that same love back to the Father. The Father beholds the Son; the Son beholds the Father. That is, the beholding is radiated by the Father to the Son. The Son, irradiated by the Father's beholding him, now re-radiates that beholding back to the Father.

Exchange, re-exchange. Radiating, re-radiating. Reflecting, re-reflecting.

Can we find one word that sums up all this? Yes, we can. What you are seeing here is the *fellowship* of the Godhead! The exchange of Christian fellowship going on within the Godhead! Remember that. *This* is the essence of the experience of the Christian life.

In its purest, most ancient, and most primitive form, we have just seen the Christian life! All springs from this first, simple, primitive, pristine, primeval *fellowship* of the Godhead. The Christian life, in its essence, is no more—and no less—than this.

The exchange of divine life.

The *source* of the outliving of the Christian life is an exchange of divine life between the members of the Godhead.

Of course, you are a mortal not destined for such high and holy matters. You cannot possibly have any part in such a thing!

Or, can you?

Yes, you can! This *is* the Christian life, and it is not going to change. If this exchange of divine elements was central to the Trinity, if this really was the Christian life in its most ancient expression, then this is also the primary element of the Christian life today. And therefore it is central to your life as a believer.

It would follow, would it not, that this *should* be the primary pursuit of all Christendom. It ought to be, but it isn't!

Dear reader, behold the secret to the Christian life and the practical living out of the Christian life as first practiced and experienced by the Son of God in eternity past.

Now an odd thing happened one day. This ancient scene was going on within God when he entered into the physical creation. For the first time ever, the Christian life was going to be lived and experienced not only in God, not only in the eternals, but also on our planet. The *how* of the Christian life was about to be introduced to earth. One day the Christian life came here to the visible creation. The location? A region called Galilee, in a town called Nazareth.

The Son of God, who had spent all eternity fellowshiping with the Father, came to earth!

Will the simple procedure of "how to live the Christian life" change once it comes to earth? Will this radical event . . . this invasion of the Christian life into our realm . . . somehow be altered? Until now the Christian life has been lived only in the dimension of the spiritual realm. Does the visible realm, the physical creation, alter the way one lives the Christian life? Once the Christian life moves from heaven to earth, will the rules change? And what about this: The Christian life can be lived only in the spiritual realm. If that is true, how can the Christian life come to the physical realm and to this very earthly planet?

Let us see. But in the meantime, never let it be said that you do not know how the Father and the Son live the Christian life.

SEVEN

Has the Christian Life Been Altered?

Did the following scene ever take place?

"My Son, we have lived together in realms of light, here in the eternals, in perfect fellowship. But now you are going to earth. Earth is fallen, its inhabitants sinful. The Christian life can be lived *only* in the pure realm of the spirituals, in a perfect spirit. You can no longer live by my life on planet earth. When you go through that door into that other fallen realm, *all* will change! Down there you will no longer live in the fellowship of the Godhead. No, you must learn another way to live. It is not as high as the way you have known with me here. No, the way you live on earth is called the *lower* way to live the Christian life! From now on you must study your Bible every day, you must pray every day, witness, fast, tithe, speak in tongues (?), and go to church. *These* are the means by which one lives the Christian life on planet earth."

Do you think such a conversation ever took place? God forbid! When the Lord Jesus came to earth, he did pray, he did fast, and he glorified his Father (that is, he witnessed). But these things were the outward expressions—the overflow of an internal experience.*

But the question we must now face is, "Did Jesus Christ change the way he lived the Christian life once he got to earth?" Was there a radical change in the ground rules, or did *the way* remain unchanged, passing from the spiritual realm to the physical realm?

If there was a change in how he had to live the Christian life, then there are *two* ways to live the Christian life—one in the eternals and another on earth. But if there was no change, if the way remained the same, then there are several million books on this subject, and several billion sermons on this subject, that we can give away to someone we don't like!

Take a closer look at Jesus the Christian. Let us return to his youth and see what we can learn about his internal experience of living the Christian life as over against our outward performance of living the Christian life.

While Jesus Christ was growing up in Nazareth, we know that he grew physically. But, as he grew physically, he also grew spiritually. He had a spirit

---

* Did Jesus speak in tongues? I doubt it, for there is no reference to such an event in Scripture. Right now, Christendom has *overflow* and *performance* mixed up.

within him. As we learned in the companion book to this book (*The Highest Life*), his spirit belonged to the other realm. Perhaps more important, God the Father, who lives in the other realm, also lived *inside* your Lord's spirit.

It was from *within* that the Lord Jesus grew in spiritual awareness. Your Lord began sensing an indwelling Lord . . . his Father! God the Father was living in Jesus' spirit. Beyond that, he also sensed his Father's love. From within, eventually he would hear his Father speak to him—in his spirit. One day he grew to the point, spiritually, that he could behold his Father. And . . . glory, glory, glory . . . one day the fellowship of the Godhead began happening on earth . . . inside the spirit of Jesus Christ!

The Christian life is lived only in the spiritual realm. But the spiritual realm was inside the *man* named Jesus Christ. All the riches of the heavenly places were in him. He lived on this earth, but the supply of living the Christian life came from his spirit. And in mysteries we cannot understand, his spirit, though in him, is *also* in the other realm . . . the spiritual realm.

There was another radical thing (from our viewpoint, at least) that happened to Jesus. He began remembering the *past*. He recalled not just the past events of earth, such as meeting with Moses and Abraham and the prophets, but he also began remembering his past even *inside the Godhead!**

How did this happen? Jesus Christ (unlike fallen

---

* "Father, you loved me before the foundation of the world" (John 17). He began remembering eternity! In so doing, he remembered that long, rich, eternal *fellowship* that he had enjoyed with the Father before creation.

man) had a living spirit within him that was fully operational. His spirit belonged to the other realm, and in his spirit his father lived. In fact, his Father was one with his spirit. The Father *is* spirit; therefore, he lives within the sphere of the spirituals. In this case, the spiritual sphere where he resided was Jesus' spirit.

Do you think, there in Nazareth, that this carpenter named Jesus abandoned either the memory or the means of that fellowship that had been his in eternity past? No, he abandoned neither. He once again laid hold of experience he had known for eternal ages. Back there in eternity, your Lord had acquired a habit. *It was a habit he had practiced a very long time!* As long as eternity (however long that was)! The habit? *How* to live the Christian life!

Did he give up the "way" of living the Christian life that he had experienced in his Father? Did he abandon that "way" for things such as tithing, fasting, and going to the synagogue? Your Lord gave the answer himself. Listen to him tell how he lived the Christian life.

I am always hearing
the voice of my Father. (John 12:50)

I see the Father. (John 5:19; 6:46)

The Father taught me. (John 8:28)

My Father loves me, and he loves you too.
(John 15:9; 16:27)

I go to the Father. (John 16:28)

Where I am [present tense]
you cannot come. (John 7:34, 36)

The Son of Man has come from the heavenlies.
(John 3:13)

Jesus Christ brought the way to live the Christian
life out of eternity and placed it here on earth, unchanged. That "way" worked as well in Nazareth,
inside Jesus' spirit, as it did in eternity past. It
worked as well in a carpentry shop as in the very
center of God!

The Father, who lives in eternal realms and who
also lived inside the living spirit of the incarnate Son,
made it possible for the fellowship of the Godhead to
continue—to continue *here,* on earth!

Look at this fellowship from the viewpoint of geog-
raphy. Geographically, this fellowship was located in
eternity, in the eternals. There the Son of God lived
the Christian life. Geographically, he was to be found
in the Father, in spirit . . . in the spiritual realm.
Where did he live the Christian life while on earth?
In exactly the same place! Jesus Christ had a living,
functioning spirit in him. Yet, even though his spirit
was in him, his spirit also belonged to the spiritual
realm. The Father lived inside Jesus Christ. Where?
Speaking geographically, the Father lived inside the
Lord Jesus' spirit. Jesus Christ lived the Christian
life from within his spirit . . . by means of the
Father's life. Jesus Christ walked in his spirit, lived
in his spirit, and *fellowshiped* in his spirit, and it was
from that location he expressed the Christian life to
our world.

Geographically, your Lord's spirit belongs to the

other realm. That was true before creation, and that was also true when he lived in Nazareth.

The Christian life has its origin in the other realm and is always lived in the other realm. Speaking of location, you might say that Jesus Christ went into his spirit, and there he lived with the Father, and by means of the Father's life he lived the Christian life! His physical body and his human soul exhibited to the world the source and power of his divine life, which was located in his spirit. Geographically, his body and soul were on earth, but his spirit was one with the Father in heavenly places. This is where he lived the Christian life.

His way of living the Christian life was (1) to go to his Father's life, located in his spirit, (2) to draw upon that life, and (3) to allow that life to express itself in this realm, through his soul and body. The engine had not changed. The *means* of living the Christian life had not changed. The engine of the Christian life was still his Father's life . . . in Christ. Neither had the *place* changed. The *place* was "in spirit." Yes, outwardly the scenery had changed, in the sense that the outliving of the Christian life was now in an earthly setting rather than a spiritual setting.

If that was Jesus' way of living the Christian life, then what might *your* way be? Are the basics the same, or did the rules of the game change when the Christian life was passed down to you and me? Do you have a living spirit? Does that spirit belong to the other realm? Does the highest life reside in your spirit? Does Jesus Christ indwell your spirit?

Let us see the Lord's experience unfold even further.

To this point we have seen only three Christians
. . . the Trinity, in the eternals before creation! Then
in about the year 4 B.C., one member of the Trinity
came out of the invisibles, exhibiting the outliving of
the Christian life for us here on earth—before people,
for us to behold. The fellowship of the Godhead entered into a kind of "stage two." And nothing changed
from stage one to stage two, except the backdrop!

Then, in about A.D. 26, twelve men in a region
called Galilee began to see the Christian life up close.
But those twelve men are fallen. For sure, they are
not part of the Godhead. They never will be, either.
But they do live with the "second" Christian. (And
they will see the "first" Christian and the "third"
Christian—the Holy Spirit—working in him.) You
might add that the twelve want very much to become
Christians, if that is allowed. Can they? If the un-
likely answer to that is yes, will there be a major
change in the Christian life when it reaches these
twelve men? Will the rules change? Or will the *way*
remain the same?

EIGHT

Jesus Christ's Ultimate Secret

At first the twelve were attracted by his miracles, and there were a great many miracles. That is exactly where many people *stop* looking . . . signs, wonders . . . power with God! Is that where you are? Gradually the twelve were further attracted by his teachings, because his teachings were mind-boggling. Many also stop there, just learning his doctrine. Is doctrine and teaching where you are?

Dear reader, if you are enamored only with power or teaching, you will almost certainly neither get to know your Lord intimately, nor will you ever clearly see his purpose.

But little by little, the followers of Jesus took note of the *main* point: who he was . . . *and* that there was someone living inside him! They began watching the *internal* aspect of Jesus—the "within." They began to discover that *within* this person was also a *way.*

At last it dawned on the twelve men just how different he really was. He was *biologically* different, that is, he had aspects of a nature they did not have.*

The explanation for the miracles, the teachings he gave his followers, and the answers he gave his enemies all came to have an explanation in his biological composition. The explanation of this incredible creature lay *within* him. The men following him began seeing him on a new level. Unlike them, he had God living in him! His "secret" lay within him.

Light broke. Power, teachings, and all outward things dimmed. They began to see that something was going on *inside* this Jesus that had to do with his *Father.* Toward the end, they realized that this One operating within their Lord was what had attracted them all along!

Jesus Christ, in drawing the attention of the twelve to his Father, had succeeded in his call and his mission: He had glorified his Father among people!

It was John who seemed to have been made aware of how Jesus Christ lived the Christian life more than any other person. John was very taken up with this relationship of the Father and the Son. That intimate fellowship going on inside Jesus Christ captivated him. He came to realize that Jesus Christ drew his whole life and "outliving" from his Father. John was

---

* For an extended discussion of the nature of Jesus and this special use of the term *biologically,* see The Highest Life by Gene Edwards. One of those twelve men, John by name, would tell us that he had a higher life form in him. That higher form of life had a name: Eternal Life. John added that this One whom they were following around had come to give *them* Eternal Life. He had come to make those men *similar to him,* biologically.

so taken with this wonderful fact that he wrote an entire book about it!

What did John see? What was it that all twelve of those men saw?

The Father abides in me and I in him.

I perceive things that are from above.

I hear my Father speak.

I know those whom my Father has chosen to believe.

I saw the other realm open.

My Father is with me, I am never alone.

My Father constantly bears witness to me.

My Father sent me here from out of the other realm.

My Father is in me and he is doing the work.

I *know* the Father.

I am one with my Father.

I see God.

I live by the Father.

I have *life* in me because of him.

Without the Father, I can do nothing.

That which is of the Father
radiates out to (and becomes the experience of)
the Son.

I and my Father are so one that,
when you meet me, you meet my Father!

These elements combined to become the ultimate attraction of their Lord to the twelve. Should this not be the number-one attraction you see in Christ? Beyond eschatology, doctrine, power, evangelism, service, miracles, beyond *all* things . . . we are at last drawn *here* . . . that is, *if* we are seekers . . . if we continue to be those who are questers after him. (But if you seek merely the *external* things he offered, that is a different matter.)

If you take the things Jesus Christ spoke concerning his relationship with the Father and put them all together, then you begin to see your Lord revealing to you the fellowship going on within the Godhead. He is also letting you see what was being experienced, bodily and visibly, *inside* himself every day in Galilee. *This* is what the disciples began to realize. They realized that they actually stood in the presence of this incredible fellowship of the Godhead every day. Join them, dear reader, in that realization.

Jesus Christ was a Christian and had been a Christian, living the Christian life, for all eternity past. *This* Christian came to our realm. This visitor from the other realm was the only person on this planet with an indwelling Father, and he was the only one who *fellowshiped* with the Father. He alone, among all the inhabitants of this planet, knew the fellowship of the Godhead. He was the only one who was in on that secret—the very wellspring of the Christian life. Would he share this secret? Would he dare to enlarge the boundaries of this fellowship?

Would he allow the twelve to be included? Until now, this fellowship had been the exclusive territory of three persons: the Father, Son, and Holy Spirit. Would this incredible experience now be shared with others? Would ordinary men be allowed to touch what only God had known? Would there be a stage *three?*

Let us ask the twelve.

NINE

Questers

Did the following scene take place? (If it didn't, a lot of people *think* it did.)

The Lord Jesus calls Simon Peter aside to talk to him privately. "Simon Peter, I am about to return to the other realm. There are some things we need to get straight before I leave.

"When I lived in my Father before I came here, he and I had a unique relationship together. Then I came to earth. Nothing changed; the Father and I simply continued living out the same relationship we had experienced in eternity. My Father continued supplying me with all of his life source. I lived by his life. While here on earth, he lived in me. We fellowshiped together each day by means of his indwelling. Peter, you understand all of that was for *me*. This is

53

my secret to living the Christian life. But, Simon Peter, I want you to get this clear! All that was for me is *not* for you! *You are fallen.* You, Simon Peter, *you* must live the Christian life by other means than I do. Do you understand this? None of this living by my Father's life. None of this indwelling Lord. Certainly never think, not for a moment, that you will be invited to join in the fellowship between my Father and me.

"The secret to the Christian life for you, Peter? Well, you have to live the Christian life by your own efforts. First of all (and above everything else), you have to live a good life. Watch out how you behave and how you dress. Do good. Be nice. Next, stop sinning. That is the heart of all I came to accomplish, to stop people from sinning so much! So quit your sinning! When tempted, bow your neck and determine not to sin. Next, you have to pray. Pray hard and long . . . every day. On your knees with no cushion or carpet under your knees. Pray on a nice hard floor; that is the best way to pray. The Christian life for you is grunt, grit, and gumption. Read your Bible. Spend lots and lots of time in the Bible. Study it, study it some more, and then memorize the verses."

"Uh, excuse me Lord, I have a problem here. I cannot read. And what is a verse?"

"Never mind. Just you learn to read. Now, I know that less than one percent of the people on this planet can read; so you learn, and then you make sure the other 99 percent learn to read too. Then all of you get into the Bible."

"I am sure going to be busy, Lord!"

"Oh yes, get into some fasting, too! And tithe, and above all . . . go to church."

"Uh, Lord, what is *church?*"

"If you don't know, find out . . . start one, and make sure everyone shows up every Sunday morning at 11:00 A.M. And warn them, 'Forsake not the assembling of yourselves, as is the manner of some.'"

Is this what the Lord Jesus said to Peter? If it is, then we are all stuck with a second-class way to live the Christian life. *Some Christian life!* True, every element in that formula has merit, but *that* formula has *never,* and never will, contain the primary ingredients of the secret to the Christian life.

For the moment, let us say this really is what Jesus Christ left for us as our "survival gear." Grunt, grit, and gumption. Do you realize what this means? It means there are two ways to live the Christian life! One way for our Lord to live the Christian life, and another way for us. A first-class way to live the Christian life, reserved exclusively for, and the unshared territory of, the Godhead. Then a second-class way to live the Christian life for us peasants, one that calls for a great deal of human exertion and *outward* performance. That's it! The outward things become all-important. Performance is everything. Pleasing God, or trying to, by outward displays! The inward means little.

Or is it the other way around? Do the Father and Son live the Christian life the way *we* have been taught to live it? Do the Lord Jesus and God the Father live the Christian life by fasting, Bible study, tithing, praying, and attending church at 11:00 A.M. every Sunday morning? I doubt it!

Something is amiss around here somewhere!

Your Lord has a deep, abiding *internal* walk. But our way? Is it summed up in the cliché "Pray and read your Bible every day or you may not make it"? Pity the poor fellow who misses a day, and yet greater pity for the Christian who is illiterate!

Take your choice. Each of us must choose what will be our central concentration: an indwelling Lord or an objective, outward performance; fellowshiping with him or trying to make him happy by being good and doing lots of nice things. We really do not have any other options! Speaking personally, I have tried both, and there is no comparison. (Fortunately, you can make your decision based on empirical experimentation, as we shall see later.) Which sounds more sane? Which looks like it has the fingerprints of Jesus Christ all over it?

His closest followers chose the way of an indwelling Lord and fellowship with that Lord. For them, it was no choice at all because they had never even heard of the other way. And no wonder. "Pray and read your Bible" as the secret to the Christian life had not even been invented yet.

Let us see just what came about as a result of the choice the twelve made.

TEN

The Re-radiating of the Christian Life

The Lord's closest followers all watched Jesus Christ live by his Father's life. These men bore witness that their Lord had told them the way he had lived by the Father in the Godhead was also the way he lived the Christian life on earth.

After Jesus died and rose again, the Holy Spirit came to live inside these men. He also spoke inside these men, and loved inside these men, and reminded them of those things Jesus said, and reminded them of *how* he lived. *These men began to live the Christian life the same way Jesus did!* That was the result of a choice they made: either to live by externals or by fellowship with an indwelling Lord. What will be your choice?

Please forever hold this incredible truth in your

heart, for it holds the embryo of all we need to know about *how* to live the Christian life. *What the Father was to Jesus Christ, so Jesus Christ had become to his disciples . . . an indwelling Lord.*

The Father lived in Jesus Christ as his very life and his daily living. Later, after the resurrection, Jesus became the very life and living of his disciples.

The number of participants in this incredible fellowship had enlarged. A small group of human beings was let in! This time radiating and re-radiating . . . reflecting and re-reflecting . . . was going on not only between Jesus Christ and the Father. Now the twelve were receiving and returning!

What did they receive? Why, the same thing they returned! Divine life. Love. Hearing. Speaking. Beholding . . . the interchange and intra-exchange of fellowship.

But never get the idea that such an incredible experience would broaden to also include *you* and *me!* It all stopped right there.

Or did it?

Listen to what the Lord's followers reported to be *his* main point. Note that everything he says here is a description of his fellowship with the Father and the Holy Spirit. Also note that he is passing on this same relationship to ordinary people. Radiating and re-radiating!

The Holy Spirit is with you and shall be *in* you.
(The Holy Spirit is in me.)

I will not leave you, I will come to you.
(The Father has never left me.)

The world will not see me anymore,
but *you* will *behold* me.

I am in my Father
My Father is in me

And you are in me
and I am *in you*.
(Stage one, two, *and* three.)

You are a branch growing out of me.
I abide in you.

I came forth from the Father.
Father, everything I have and all that I am is from
you.

Father, we are one. Let *them* now be one,
in the same way that *we* are one.
(Re-radiating.)

They are not from this realm,
just as I am not from this realm.

I ask for them, and for those who come after them,
who believe what they say.

Father, you are in me.
I am in you. We are one.
Add to the oneness—
that all those you gave me
may be one with one another,
and that they may be *in* us.
(Stage one, two, and three, sharing with one
another.)

You gave me glory.
In the same way, I have given *them* glory!

You are in me.
I am in them (passing on the experience,
Father to Son, Son to disciples).

Father, love them in the very same way you love
me.

I beheld your glory.
Then you gave me glory.
Now I return to you, Father.
May they whom you gave me . . .
may they also be where I am,
that they may behold my glory.
Let them see the very glory I had
before the foundation of the world.

The love with which you loved me is inside me.

Now let that love be inside them . . .
let your love be in them in exactly the same way
that I am in them!
(The fellowship now includes *people;*
God has set no restrictions on stage three.)

What you have just read is what these men reported as the main issue of Jesus' heart. Now listen
to what those men reported as the main issue of *their*
hearts.

He was there at the very beginning,
yet I also heard him.
I even saw him.

And whom I beheld I also touched
with my very own hands! Life himself!

He who is eternal life,
this very One I now declare *him* . . . to you.
He was with the Father in eternity past.
Then he was with us.
Now I proclaim him to you.
Why? So that you may have fellowship
with those of us who have fellowshiped with him.

And who is it we fellowship with . . . today?
Though he ascended and went back into the Father,
he is still *here.*
And every day I still fellowship
with the Father and with his Son,
even though I am on earth.

Fill up your joy.
Come fellowship with us.

I abide in him.
My walk is in him.
I am walking in him in the same manner
he walked with the Father.

Let him, of whom you have heard,
now abide in you.
Then you will abide in the Son
and you will abide in the Father.

The anointing also dwells in you and teaches you.

You know he dwells in you
by means of the Spirit, whom he has given you.

The One who is in you is greater
than the one who is in the world.

God sent his *only* begotten Son into the world
so that *you* might live by *him.*

We are in him who is true.
The Truth abides *in* you and will forever.

You were born from above by a living hope.
You have been born from above by an imperishable
Seed.
That Seed, which is *in you,*
is he who is the living and abiding Word of God.

Set apart Christ in your heart;
there, let him be Lord.

Be ready to give a word concerning the hope *in you.*

His divine power has granted you *everything
that has to do with life and godliness.*

You have become a partaker
of the *divine* nature.

Having looked at what the Lord said, and what his
closest disciples said, you and I living in the twentieth century must ask ourselves: Did this higher way
to live the Christian life end with the twelve? Can
you dare to believe:

What the Father was to Jesus Christ, so
Jesus Christ is to you . . . an indwelling
Lord!

ELEVEN

Stage Four

Do you think the following conversation ever took place?

Peter is speaking.

"Now listen up, you three thousand. I am only going to say this once. There are two kinds of Christians: those of us who live the Christian life by the same means Jesus Christ lived the Christian life . . . and then there is *you!* We apostles are in on this first way . . . and then there is you. You are second-class Christians! *You* do *not* get the same equipment the Lord Jesus had, or that we have. You are peasants. Do you understand? You are to struggle. Did you hear me? *Struggle!* Grunt! Grit! Strain! Bow your neck! Use your will, your best effort! Fast. And pray (preferably on your knees on a hard floor with no carpet).

"As for John and me and all the rest of us twelve, we lived with him for over three years. We got to see firsthand how *he* lived the Christian life. But you did not. Remember that. *You* only get to know about all these wonderful things *secondhand,* so that puts you in a lower class. We twelve refer to all of you as 'underclass Christians.'

"We lived with him. He dwells within us just like the Father dwelt within him. The secret to the Christian life, for *us,* is that we live by a Lord who indwells us. But that is *us, not* you. What, then, do you have to do to live the victorious Christian life? There is *no way* to pass on to you what *we* have. So, here is *your* way to live the Christian life.

"First, it is required of you that you learn to read, pray (preferably on your knees, etc.). And tithe (remember to tithe; otherwise God will not like you). And go to Sunday school. Oh yes, today I, Simon Peter, am going to invent something called *church.* Now church is not the community of the believers; it is not a twenty-four-hour-a-day way of living; the church is not a people. No sir! And it is not exciting, vital, vibrant, something that will win your heart and soul. Nor is it a beautiful girl, a bride for the Lord Jesus. No, the church is simply a building—a brick building with hard seats in it—the harder the better. You must report to this building promptly at 11:00 A.M. every Sunday morning. (Not 10:00 A.M. or 9:00 A.M. or 3:00 P.M., or Friday, or Saturday, or some evening, but 11:00 A.M. on Sunday). Make it any other time and you are some kind of a cult. And when you go in, sit down and be quiet. Do not become an actual participant. Do whatever the bulletin tells you to do. Nothing more. The rest of the time just sit and listen! Listen to a droning (maybe even incomprehensible) sermon. Do not get sleepy and do not talk to anyone. And surely, for my sake (that is, for Pete's sake), do not speak, do not share. I repeat: Do *not* participate. Just sit! Understand? Sit! Stay awake. And if you can understand what is being said, *listen.*

"As I said, church is not a way of living, it is a one-hour-a-week ritual. And you had better show up for it every Sunday for the rest of your life, because doing that is the main secret to the Christian life. Forget *koinonia;* think ritual! Do all these things, or God and I won't like you, and you will never be able to be a good Christian.

"Sooo . . . pray, read your Bible. (We promise to get it written as soon as possible. You might even have a chance to own a copy by about A.D. 300 if you're still alive and have lots of money.) Fast, go to church, tithe, and a few other things I will tell you about later when I am in a bad mood. Oh yes, and speak in tongues. Like the hundred and twenty did yesterday. By the way, I want you to know I was very disappointed in all three thousand of you at Pentecost yesterday. Not one of you three thousand spoke in tongues. Just think, the day of Pentecost and three thousand of you did not speak in tongues! We are obviously off to a bad start. You must try harder."

Did this happen? No? Then why, pray tell, do we act like it did?

Was the above formula imparted to the three thousand as the secret to the Christian life? And is this what is expected of all the rest of us Christians who will come after them?

Is this our fate? Is this the prescription for living the Christian life for everyone who came *after* the apostles? Are you cut off from the fellowship of the Godhead? Can you never know what Jesus Christ knew about how to live the Christian life? Can we not enter into *his* experience? If "read your Bible, go to church, and pray" is *the* foundation of the Christian life, then where is the touch of the divine in living out the Christian life? Do we get an intimate touch with a divine Lord *only* at the moment of salvation? Is an intimate, daily walk with Jesus Christ over with forever? Are we living under some new dispensation that cuts us off from him?

Take only the route presented above, and you launch out in a direction that gives you no relationship with the realm of the spirituals. Basically what these formulas are saying is: Become saved . . . that is a truly *spiritual,* other-realm, profound internal *experience. But* after that the Christian life is all grit, groan, and grunt. For you, the divine touch, the walk with the Spirit in your spirit, and intimacy with Jesus Christ are nonexistent.

Recently a professor of theology in one of our most respected seminaries was lecturing to his class from a point of view so extreme that it virtually dethroned God and enthroned the Bible in place of God. One of his students asked, "But what about an indwelling Lord?" Listen to the professor's response: "The only way we know the Lord indwells us is that the Bible tells us he does." Are we really that far removed from the reality of Christ?

Maybe, just maybe, we really have missed the main point.

Well, dear reader, that professor's view of how to live the Christian life is on about the same level as "how to live the Muslim life," or "how to live the Hebrew life." Where is that which is truly unique to the Christian? Where is a personal relationship to a living Lord? Remove that element, and we are Christians who are consigned to live our daily lives on about the same spiritual level as a Hebrew or a Muslim. A living, indwelling Lord is the "something" we have that no other religion on earth can offer. In fact, other religions never dreamed of offering such glory. Jesus Christ offers access to personal fellowship with our God. Are we on the verge of abrogating *that?!*

The secret to the Christian life is first found in what went on in the Godhead in eternity. The second great illustration and expression of the secret to the Christian life comes to us in Jesus Christ. His way can be summed up in what was going on inside himself while working in a carpentry shop. Look *there* for the secret to the Christian life!

The third illustration of this secret is found in the early disciples and in their personal testimony of a vital relationship and a *continuing* fellowship with an indwelling Lord.

Behold the Godhead; behold Jesus Christ in a carpentry shop; behold twelve men; hear their testimony about their fellowship with the Father and the Son as they raise up the first ecclesia.

Take any other starting point and you will end up with something terribly off course, incredibly short of the mark, indescribably shallow, totally unworkable, and probably just a hair away from humanism—not to mention a Christian life based wholly on the concept that we have to make God happy and that we have to do that by performance and outward good works.

Did he who *began* deep in your spirit switch over to physical effort? Do we, who began our first moment as Christians in our spirit, then switch over to the frontal lobe and to willpower?

Look under the facade of any "secret" to the Christian life that does not begin with the *eternal* relationship of the Father and the Son *and* the *earthly* relationship of the Father and the Son. What you are apt to find is not much more than a bootstrap religion.

The three thousand *were* told about Jesus' relationship to his indwelling Father. The twelve apostles, standing in front of three thousand new believers, told them of their own experience with a Lord who had been physically present with them and who was now *in* them . . . and of their own present relationship to that *indwelling* Lord.

These men revealed to the three thousand a new dimension of living. These twelve church planters opened a door through which three thousand individuals in the ecclesia could step into the realm of the spirit. (They heard "walk in the spirit," and it made perfect sense to them and became experiential in their lives.) This other-realm aspect of the lives of all the believers bore no resemblance to what was being passed off as "the secret" to the Hebrew life. It was utterly unlike anything presented in the Jerusalem temple by Hebrew theologians, nor did it resemble anything ever known, taught, or espoused in any other religion at any time in all human history.

The twelve explained to the three thousand about their now living daily by his life, about being able to hear him inside, about sensing him, loving him, *beholding* him, and most of all . . . fellowshiping with him . . . *within.*

Those twelve men, formerly enslaved to (and now freed from) one of the world's most objective religions, did not suddenly share an objective, surface gospel. Those twelve men were proclaiming a whole new dimension that had never been known nor dreamed of. They proclaimed that a living God had moved inside the believer, was inside them right then, *living the Christian life.* That is the gospel the three thousand heard, and that is the gospel the three thousand new believers came to experience together in hundreds of homes all over the city of Jerusalem. The number-one trait of the first ecclesia was that of believers *corporately* experiencing Jesus Christ *in community.*

Ah, but it all ended there, did it not? All the Christians who came *after* the birth of the ecclesia in Jerusalem—they got stuck with a frontal-lobe Christianity and a noncommunity, church-at-11:00 A.M. Christian life. Is that not true?

What about all us "later-on" believers? What, for instance, was the secret to the Christian life as proclaimed to all those unclean, uncircumcised Gentile believers way up there hundreds of miles north of Jerusalem in the pagan land of Galatia?

Let us take a look at some of the believers who never personally lived with the Lord, who never met the twelve apostles and (until they got saved) had been illiterate, sexually immoral, blood-drinking *infidels!* Just what did *they* understand the secret to the Christian life to be?

TWELVE

The Gentile Secret

Paul of Tarsus is speaking to a living room full of recently converted heathen in Galatia. Talk about a man with problems to solve! Talk about a man with new concepts to communicate in an impossible environment!

These ex-heathen heard the word *prayer,* but it was a foreign concept to them! The concept of a tithe meant nothing to these people, but for a reason you could never guess: Most of them had never seen money. Money was a foreign concept because most of these Galatians lived by bartering goods. Bartering was the main means of exchange. Most of the people in that room *never* touched money in the course of a year. Nor could these people understand "Go to church." Church buildings did not exist, and they would not exist for another three hundred years. Even the local heathen temples were built in such a way that people stood *outside* the pagan temple to watch the ritual of temple worship. So going *into* a building to worship would have been an odd concept to them. Finally, if fifty to one hundred people were present in this living room, no more than five or six of them could read. Even if they *had* been literate, there was nothing to read. The idea of books being produced in large quantities had never crossed the mind of Gentiles any more than it had Hebrews. The average Gentile in the average town of Galatia might never see a book in his entire lifetime. The overwhelming majority of the population of the region of Galatia stood barely one rung above abject slavery.

What gospel could possibly become relevant to these people? Only one! A primitive gospel, experienced by the Trinity, brought to earth *in Christ,* and experienced and passed on by men who planted the ecclesia . . . only *that* gospel would fit the needs of *all* these people. These ex-infidels would live in the ecclesia planted by Paul. There in that community of believers they would help one another, see one another daily, meet together, and know Christ together. That is, they would come to know an indwelling Lord in the same way those three thousand new Hebrew converts back in Jerusalem had come to know Christ intimately.

Would the gospel preached to these Gentiles by church planters such as Paul be the gospel of (1) go to church, (2) read your Bible, (3) pray, (4) tithe, (5) be good, (6) fast, and (7) speak in tongues? Or would it be to know, meet, encounter, experience, and embrace a living, indwelling Lord . . . daily . . . and *corporately?*

Let us take Paul's letters in the order in which they were written and *see* what the secret to the Christian life was to Paul. Let us see what gospel he unfolded to these illiterate people . . . people who had been worshipers of stone idols, and people steeped in the local lores of superstition just a few days earlier. What you find in these letters Paul wrote is what you find being experienced in the lives of his converts. What, pray tell, did those ex-heathen hear from Paul, anyway? What did they understand the secret to the Christian life to be?

As we look into Paul's correspondence with these people, keep this in mind. These letters were all written, not to individuals, but to an *ecclesia,* the "colony of heaven," the community of believers. Point: Spiritual reality is first to and for the *ecclesia,* not to and for the *individual.* Believers back in those days understood the Christian life only in the context of a close-together living of the Christian life. The Christian life and the ecclesia were virtually the same thing to these people.

The secret to the Christian life is Christ. The secret to the practical aspects of knowing him is found in daily church life!

Here, then, we have a thought that is just about unknown to present-day evangelical believers. The Christian life really is not for the individual believer; it is not for any of us *outside* the context of the koinonia (fellowship) of the ecclesia. Or, at least, we must say that the Christian life was never *intended* to be lived outside the community of the redeemed.

The ecclesia and the daily living of the Christian life are inseparable. Therefore, as you hear Paul's words to the Gentiles, note that his words are incredibly spiritual, yet delivered in a world where 98 percent of the people were either slaves or one cut above slaves, and where illiteracy was running over 98 percent, and where *ecclesia* and Christian were virtually synonymous in the daily lives of the believers. Try to remember that his words were addressed to the *community* of the redeemed.

The Letter to the Galatians

The word *in* was central in the vocabulary of the Gentile Christians. (*In* means union with, oneness with, Christ.)

Christ is *inside* the believer. (1:16)

Faith in Christ is central. (2:16)

Believers cannot successfully obey
rules, commands, or ordinances,
and neither can anyone else. (2:14, 19)

A Christian is dead, and Christ lives in his place.
The believer lives by another life form, a higher life.
Christ is that higher life . . .
the believer lives by him. (2:20)

The Christian begins the Christian life
by receiving an indwelling Spirit.
He lives by that Spirit,
and his whole Christian walk is by that Spirit
and by nothing else . . . certainly not
by rules, regulations, and commands. (3:2-3)

A man who has become truly righteous
has become righteous by faith.
It is this man who has *life!* (3:11)

Living by rules, regulations, rituals,
traditions, laws, and commands
will never give you the life of God,
whose life alone can live the Christian life. (3:21)

There is a family that has
the highest life on the biological chart.
All members of that family have the life of God in
them.
They live by the same life that God lives by.
You belong to that family. (3:26; 4:5)

You are inside Christ.
(You cannot get much more *in* than that!) (3:27)

The very Spirit of Jesus Christ
is in the believer's spirit. (4:6)

God experientially knows you,
and you experientially know him. (4:9)

Christ lives in you and is being formed in you. (4:19)

You loose-living Gentiles,
dare you be told that you are absolutely free
from all rules and laws? (4:31; 5:1, 13)

You are led by your internal, spiritual parts.
You can live by the Spirit. (5:16, 18)

Your spirit effortlessly produces fruit.
Fruit that you have to struggle to produce

is not fruit; it is work . . .
work produced by the flesh. (5:22)

You are a biologically new species.
You have parts in you the unbeliever does not have.
You are internally different from the unsaved.
It is not works of law nor ordinances
that are important to God or to you.
God is in your spirit.
Works are in the flesh. (5:24; 6:18)

Plow your spirit today,
and today eternal life will spring up! (6:8)

And now, let us go to the Greek world, where the believers were very much like the Galatian believers as far as money, education, and living conditions were concerned.

Thessalonians
The word *in* is still there!

The Lord alone causes you to love. (1 Thess. 3:12)

God put his very Holy Spirit inside you. (4:8)

God teaches you how to love others
in the local ecclesia. (4:9)

It was Light that birthed you
and Day that is your Father.
We are of Light and Day. (5:5, 8)

As an ecclesia, we live with the Lord. (5:10)

He called you. He will keep you. (5:24)

One day he who is in us
will burst forth out of us . . . in glory! (2 Thess. 1:10)

There will be a visible, physical appearance
of him who is *already* present.
It is the Lord himself
who turns your heart to loving God
and to Christ's own steadfastness. (2:8, 13-15)

Now let us go to those wild Gentiles in Corinth.

Corinthians

It is not by the eye gate,
nor the ear gate nor the thinking gate,
that a believer *knows.*
*God reveals to you through his Spirit
into* your spirit. (1 Cor. 2:10)

Only your spirit, deep inside you,
really knows all that God has given you. (2:12; 6:19)

The Spirit of God himself dwells in you. (3:16)

Spiritual things can be sown inside a believer. (9:11)

There is actually spiritual food,
and a believer can partake of that food,
and that food is Christ. (10:1-4)

The church is the visible body
of an invisible but present Lord. (chapter 12)

Jesus Christ gives his Spirit to you,
and his Spirit gives you his life.
That *life* has its origins in another realm. (15:47)

We are heavenly beings because

we were born in the heavenlies.
The most important part of you, your spirit,
was born in and remains in the other realm.
(15:44-49)

His Spirit is in your heart. (2 Cor. 1:22)

The Spirit of God *writes* on your heart. (3:3)

The Spirit gives you God's own life. (3:6)

The believer can see the unseen! (4:18)

You are in Christ
and you are a biologically unique species,
different *internally* from the unbeliever. (5:17)

The power of Christ himself dwells in the believer.
(12:9)

Jesus Christ is in you. (13:5)

And now, let us go to those hot-blooded Italians in
Rome!

Romans

True circumcision is within. (2:29)

Things which do not exist . . . exist! (4:17)

You are saved through his life. (5:10)

You are in Christ and therefore alive to God (6:11)

The Spirit of Life (the Highest Life) is in you. (8:2)

God's Spirit dwells in you. (8:9)

Christ's Spirit dwells in you. (8:9)

Christ himself is in you. (8:10)

The Father dwells in you. (8:11)

You are led by the Lord from the inside,
by the indwelling Spirit. (8:14)

God fellowships with you in your spirit. (8:15-16)

You are weak, but the indwelling Spirit

in you is not weak. (8:26)

God's love is in Christ,
and you are in Christ too.
You and the love of God are both in Christ. (8:39)

God is able to make you stand. (14:4)

And what of the believers in an area sometimes
called Asia Minor?

Ephesians

By means of the Father
you have access to the spiritual riches
in the other realm. (1:3)

Right now in your spirit
you are seated with Christ
in the other realm. (2:6)

You had your origin inside Christ Jesus. (2:10)

By means of the Spirit
you can go directly to the Father. (2:18)

The Father is in you. (4:6)

As a redeemed Gentile
you have the life of God. (4:17-20)

You have *heard* Christ speaking in you,
and he has taught you. (4:20-21)

Jesus Christ causes the *ecclesia*
to live the Christian life—hurrah! (5:23-32)

His strength is your strength. (6:10)

All of you (the church),
put on the armor of God. (6:11-12)

Go inside where the Lord dwells,
in your spirit, to pray. (6:18)

Colossians

You are filled with all spiritual wisdom. (1:9)

He who is in you
has all treasures in himself,
and the fullness of the Father is in him. (1:19; 2:2-3)

The mystery: Christ in you. (1:27)

The Godhead, in all fullness,
dwells in Christ Jesus—
visibly—in bodily form.
And you are filled with him
for you are in him. (2:9-10)

It is a speaking Lord who dwells in you. (3:16)

Philippians

There is enormous supply in Christ's Spirit. (1:19)

Getting to know Christ Jesus personally and
internally
is the most unsurpassable of all values. (3:8)

Because you are from the other realm,
your citizenship is also in that realm. (3:20)

All your supply for all your needs
is in an indwelling Lord. (4:19)

Where in all these magnificent words to these very
poor, uneducated Gentile is the cliché "Pray and read
your Bible" to be a good Christian?

A whole different feel about our relationship to
Christ is found in these epistles. What we see here is
a group of former heathen who have a deep, internal
relationship with the Lord Jesus Christ. In these
letters, *that relationship is taken for granted.* And
that relationship is being experienced among these
believers *daily.*

One of the most telling points about these letters is
how they all begin. They begin by establishing the
relationship between the Father and the Son. *All* of
them! (See Rom. 1:7; 1 Cor. 1:2-4; 2 Cor. 1:2-3; Gal.
1:3; Eph. 1:2-3ff.; Phil. 1:2; Col. 1:2-3; 1 Thess. 1:3;
2 Thess. 1:1-2.)

Much of all that follows thereafter is an invitation
to the ecclesia (simple, ordinary believers) to join in
and become part of that relationship.

Is a pattern emerging here?

Go back through eternity past, then through the
whole of the first century, and see *one* unbroken line.
One common wellspring, one common denominator
among all those involved in the Christian walk. And

when I say all, that includes the Father, the Son, the apostles, the wealthy, the middle-class, and the vast majority of believers, . . . the illiterate, Gentile share-croppers and slaves living in dirty little towns in the dingiest, poorest parts of Galatia and in the slums of Greece, Asia Minor, and Rome.

But that was Century One. What about believers in Century Twenty-One?

THIRTEEN

John's Suggestion

It is about five o'clock on Monday morning. Yesterday was Pentecost. Peter has called a meeting of all the three thousand new converts at six o'clock this morning. But he has asked the other eleven apostles to meet with him before that meeting. The purpose of the rendezvous, to take place on the wall overlooking Solomon's court, is to discuss their plans for the day.

The twelve apostles all arrive. Peter poses a question, "What on earth are we going to tell these people? What is the first thing we should tell them? If the Lord were here today, what would we tell them? What is a good introduction to new converts?"

Judas (not Iscariot) raises his hand. "Well, Peter, I have been working on this wall chart on the thirteen dispensations of eschatology. It is mostly from the books of Ezekiel and Lamentations."

"How about a theological dissertation on the seven deadly virtues?" chimes in Didymus.

"Just because he is one of the only three of us who can read, he thinks everything has got to be intellectual," mutters Matthew.

"I think we ought to talk about the seven steps to effective prayer rather than the seven deadly virtues," adds Simeon.

"That is not what they need. What they need is to be told about the fivefold gifts of the soul," counters Andrew.

"I think we ought to teach them to read their Bible and go to church," says Thaddeus.

"What's a Bible?" asks Simon Peter. "Oh, never mind. Whatever it is, you have to remember, Thaddeus, I cannot read. And as to your other suggestion, what did you say? Teach them to go to a *what?*"

Peter turns to James. "James, what do you think we ought to do?"

"Don't you go looking at me, Simon Peter. You are our leader, not me!"

For a long moment Simon Peter sits quietly. He knows it is almost time to go down and begin sharing with those three thousand people. He peeps up over the battlements of the wall, stares for a brief moment, and sinks down to the floor. He expresses his feelings in one word.

"Oooh . . . !"

James peeks over the wall, sees three thousand eager faces and moans, "Oh no . . . oh no! Doesn't someone know what to do?"

All during this time John has been very quiet, but at this point, he raises his hand. "Peter, I have an idea. What do you think about this?

We have seen Jesus Christ,
we have heard Jesus Christ.
We have touched him,
we have been with him,
we have fellowshiped with him.
But then he died,
and we did not have him.
Later he rose,
and after he arose, he ascended.
Now he indwells each one of us.
The fellowship we once had with him still continues.

"Let us tell these three thousand new believers about how twelve men, as a group, knew him and now experience him. Let us show them how to be with the Lord Jesus Christ and how to intimately experience him . . . just as we do. After they have touched him, known him, and had fellowship with him, then they will understand our experience, and they will understand our words. The new believers will know . . . experientially . . . how to walk with him and fellowship with him; then they will be able to fellowship with him; then they will be able to fellowship with us just as you and I fellowship with the Lord Jesus Christ every day."

Peter takes in John's every word, sits silently for a moment, and then replies, "John, would you say that again . . . a little more briefly this time."

John takes a deep breath.

The One whom we have seen
and heard and touched—
let us declare him unto them
that they might have fellowship with us.
After all, our fellowship is with the Father
and with the Son, the Lord Jesus Christ.

And so the twelve disciples walk down into Solomon's porch and tell what it is like to have fellowship with the God-Man, Jesus Christ. Then they tell how they continue having fellowship with him since he came inside of them as a living, indwelling Lord.

Having shared this incredible word, the twelve then *show* the three thousand how to have fellowship with Jesus Christ, who is also living in each one of them. By that means the three thousand discover how to fellowship with the Lord . . . within. Then what happens? The three thousand understand the things the twelve were telling them about an indwelling Lord and understood what is going on inside of the twelve.

Then it came to pass that the three thousand also began fellowshiping with one another about their fellowship with the Lord! In so doing, there came into existence a living fellowship that had once belonged only to the Father, the Son, and the Holy Spirit but now belonged also to three thousand, one hundred and twenty! And the more they fellowshiped with one another, the more they understood the twelve and the more they were able to fellowship with them, with the Lord, *and* with one another.

All this fellowship redounded to the glory of the

Father, and to his Son, the Lord Jesus Christ. Oh, yes, and also to the Bride, the church!

But this wonder of all wonders did not end with the Trinity nor the twelve nor the three thousand believers.

You have a right to enter into that same fellowship with the Godhead and with fellow believers in the ecclesia. It is yours . . . an experience as real and as intimate as that which was experienced by the early believers within the ecclesia.

FOURTEEN

The Secret to the Christian Life . . . Spectacularly Overlooked

This chapter has a simple purpose, to tear your thinking loose from some of the prominent evangelical thinking of this era. The evangelical mind-set is very *individualistic* in nature, very *I-centered,* very objective. It is a mind-set virtually void of the centrality of Christ and the centrality of the ecclesia in the spiritual walk of the believer. Most of all, it is an outlook that is performance-oriented and steeped in the concept that if you will just try a little harder, you *can* be a good Christian. How shall we challenge such an overpowering mind-set? Perhaps by a closer look at it.

Let's collect all the sermons ever preached and put them *all* together into *one* sermon. We begin with sermons preached in the year A.D. 350 and go on collecting them right through to this last Sunday. Almost all of these messages have a common theme. Most of them are telling those of us sitting out there in the pews what we are supposed to do to be good Christians.

Having made all these sermons into one gigantic sermon, we now have a message so long that it would tax the storage capacity of the world's most advanced computers! When the computer finally spewed out this incredible sermon, it would fill the largest building on earth.

How many topics are covered in that sermon? Think of all the exhortations, threats, and demands! And the lists! Endless lists of things you ought to do and not do to a good Christian. Think of the demands aimed at *you!* There would be literally millions of them.

Now imagine that you *memorize* this entire sermon! Hundreds of millions of pages memorized—by you! At last! You now know exactly what is required of you in order to be a good Christian. Just think of all the things you are supposed to do . . . today!

Now, dear reader, armed with the greatest knowledge ever poured into one brain, it is time you set out to live the Christian life! (Come on—get going!)

The alarm clock goes off at 6:00 A.M. You are already in trouble. Praying Hyde got up *all* his life at 4:00 A.M. and prayed four hours every morning. Guilt overwhelms you. John Wesley prayed all night on hundreds of occasions. More guilt. Get out of bed, you sloth!

But wait! Maybe you should lie in bed and quietly sing a song? Was not that one point in the sermon?

Or maybe you should begin your prayers in bed? Or should you throw off the covers boldly? Or gently? Or should you step out of the bed and slip humbly to your knees? Or should you stand, arms uplifted, and shout praises to God? Or maybe you should fall on your face and cry out for mercy to God for your sinful state? Should you turn on the light (and perhaps waste electricity) or pray in the dark and risk falling asleep? How long should you pray? Ten minutes? Three hours? Four hours? Standing? Kneeling? Prostrate? Eyes open? Eyes closed?

That sermon told you to do all of these things! *Every* day! And *never* fail!

Wait a minute, you slob, you have not made up your bed yet! First things first. Get your room cleaned up; God hates sloppy people. How dare you pray before you clean up your room!

At last, it is time to go to the bathroom. Should you march in there boldly as a victorious Christian, ready to take on the world; or should you walk humbly, like the pale Galilean who walked gently upon this earth?

Aha! You are out of toothpaste, and you told your wife to buy some, and she did not. Should you rebuke her? (Woman, the Bible says you must obey me in all things.) Should you forgive her and speak gently to her? Or should you, the humble one, forget the whole incident and just brush without toothpaste? Or perhaps it would be better if you did not pay any attention to such worldly things as brushing your teeth and just went around with bad breath, trusting God to keep your teeth from falling out of your head.

That sermon told you to do *all* of the above. Forget the ambiguity; do them *all*. Every day!

Well, thank goodness, there is *one* thing for certain, the entire sermon agrees that you must put on some clothes. But should you put on ritzy clothes to show people how God provides for Christians, or should you put on some worn-out old overalls, showing the world that you, the Christian, live an austere, humble, somber, and stoic life?

That sermon told you to do all of the above!

Somewhere between the time you wake up and the time you get to breakfast, you are going to have a complete nervous breakdown!

Some sermon you memorized, right? A big help to your Christian life, huh?

And by the way, you miserable sinner, you failure, you dregs of Christianity, you millstone to other believers, you poor hopeless hypocritical failure—this morning you were so busy doing everything else that sermon told you to do that you forgot to read your *Bible!* It is just as well. You never would have figured out whether you should read it inductively, deductively, didactically, or meditatively, not to mention topically or analytically. Remember, that sermon told you to do all of the above! *Every* day!

Do not forget that all Christians are supposed to read through the New Testament once every three weeks. For shame! (Or was it read the New Testament three times every week?!)

And witnessing! Witness to one lost soul every day, like Moody did. And help the poor. And attend *all* church functions. Care for your neighbors. Fast at least one day per week. Tithe 30 percent of your income like the Jews did in the Old Testament. Take a Bible correspondence course. Read one new Christian book per week. (Or was it two?) Visit the sick. Go to a prayer breakfast and a prayer dinner. Fly to Eastern Europe for a door-to-door evangelism campaign. Spend one hour a day reading to your children, *and* take them camping. Do not forget to march against bad school textbooks, listen to five daily Christian radio programs, read six Christian magazines, prepare a Sunday school lesson, support an orphan, write to a missionary, see that Christian film, attend the church picnic and the parents' retreat, do volunteer work with an interdenominational organization, go to a counseling session, and take a seminar in lay counseling.

Remember, that sermon told you to do all of the above.

Do you get the idea? Isn't something amiss in all this? Is this the Christian faith? Is this God's requirement of you for living the Christian life?

Let us move on from the world's longest sermon and try the world's biggest *book!*

Go to your nearest seminary or Bible school and take a few moments to walk up and down the aisles of their library. Virtually every book in that library is written on one simple hypothesis: Because you are saved, you can do everything all those books demand of you. All of those books presuppose that you can be a good Christian. That, dear reader, is one very awesome, and erroneous, supposition!

If we took every book written for Christians on the subject of what a good Christian is supposed to do and what he is supposed to be, and made all that into one book, surely it would be six feet high and a mile long. If you thought the world's largest sermon put you under a pile of guilt, wait until you get through reading the world's biggest Christian book—which shouldn't take you over four or five hundred years!

If you tried to do everything all those authors said you should do, you would probably go stark-raving mad in sight of a few weeks.

Now let us pile on top of that sermon and that book all the things Christian counselors tell us we are supposed to do, plus all the things all the television and radio preachers tell us to do in order to be good Christians.

Dear reader, *virtually all* of this counsel, all of those books, and every one of those sermons are setting you up for failure, for guilt, and for a lifetime of frustration.

There is only one Christian, and he alone can live the Christian life. And unless we lay hold of his life and lay hold of him, we are up against simple biology. Either we don't have the right "parts" in us to live the Christian life, or we have them but don't know it! (And that giant sermon and mammoth book aren't helping us much to find it out.)

Human beings are the wrong species for living the Christian life. Furthermore, if you were the right species, you are still the wrong person. The Christian life is . . . always has been . . . and always will be, the exclusive territory of the living God. He *alone* lives the Christian life!

I repeat, the greatest day you will ever live is the day your Lord, by revelation, shows you that you cannot live the Christian life. And if this is really a fact, then there really is a lot of unlearning and relearning to be done.

Let us move from all these do's and don'ts toward the possibility of *encounter.*

FIFTEEN

A Strong Recommendation

You threw your suitcase in the trunk of your car and drove away from one of the most glorious conferences you ever attended. But you may have become so used to hearing good preaching that you did not notice that during the entire week you really were not given any *practical* tools. Yes, you were blessed out of your socks! You heard so many glorious sermons and you got so thrilled that your toes curled up. But you did not have *anything* to take home with you but a good feeling. (As you know, that good feeling does not last very long, does it?)

Yet an intimate, personal experience with Jesus Christ . . . an experiential relationship with Jesus Christ . . . is practical. There *are* practical helps to aid you in fellowshiping with Jesus Christ. There are practical helps to aid you in getting to know him intimately.

Even such help, however, is impotent unless there is a hunger on your part—a hunger great enough to cause you to pay the price for *permanently* establishing that relationship with him. I do not know whether you fall into that category, but *you* are going to know very soon. In fact, you will know in the next few weeks!

At this point, I would like to open my heart to you about something I am genuinely afraid of as we begin to look at *practical* matters. I am quite afraid to give actual practical help to you in this book. There are several reasons for my fear, and I would like for you to know what they are.

The first reason I am reluctant to even publish this book is simple: Practical things that really work in the Kingdom of God tend to become merchandised. There is nothing holy but what some preacher out there can figure out a way to make money off of it. I fear that; I fear that possibility to the limits of my ability to fear.

I realize that not one minister in a thousand will merchandise holy things. But please note that, in the United States alone, there are over three hundred thousand Protestant ministers. That means there are about three hundred out there who will do such things! There is always someone who can figure out a way to bottle or box almost anything that has to do with the Kingdom of God.

The second reason for my concern about sharing practical help with you has to do with something I have already touched on, but it is something that is difficult to grasp fully in our day. There is one aspect of a Christian's relationship to Jesus Christ that is very sacred to me. Sacred, yes; understood, almost never.

I speak of the role of the *ecclesia* in your spiritual walk with Jesus Christ.

A large part of your personal relationship with Jesus Christ is *supposed* to be corporate and in community, *not* individual. I am not referring to your getting together with a few friends and calling that the church, nor am I talking about you and those you work with in a nondenominational organization getting together. In interdenominational movements such gatherings very often become a substitute for the ecclesia.

Nor do I speak of that verse of Scripture in Matthew 18:15ff., quoted so often as if the verse referred to something sentimental—"Where two or three are gathered, there I am in the midst of them"—with the following comment added, *"That* is the church."

No, where two or three are gathered is *not* the church! Go reread that "beautiful," "sentimental" passage again. In that verse your Lord is talking about one of the steps that is necessary to take as you move toward the point where the entire *church* excommunicates someone! Sentimental?!

Please understand that, when I speak of *corporate* or *community,* I am speaking about that which is the most holy and the most precious thing in this whole universe to your Lord. Perhaps it is not very precious to Christians today, but it is precious to God. To him, it is the most sacred element within creation. I speak of the *ecclesia.* And the ecclesia is not a thing; the ecclesia is a *she*—a bride! A visible, observable, attendable, ongoing gathering . . . the body of believers, a community of the redeemed, a colony from heaven, a nation to live in, a world within this world. Jesus Christ died for her. And it is within this *community of believers* that you are *supposed* to live, and in that community you are supposed to get to know him.

Just as it was in the first century, you and I are supposed to be saved within the sphere of the fellowship of the body of Christ. I am supposed to live out my *entire life* in a civilization called ecclesia. A community. A sacred colony. The ecclesia—she is that which captured and enraptured the first-century believers. Back then men and women found Jesus Christ as Lord and lived the rest of their entire lives together, personally, intimately, daily, *with one another.* Christ and the ecclesia were inseparable in the experience of first-century believers.

Nothing I have written here, nothing that I presently speak about, nothing I will ever preach or teach . . . *nothing* that any of us have to say about spiritual things . . . will ever work the way it is supposed to work unless it takes place within an informal, practical, living, *committed* body of believers.

I realize how difficult it is to grasp what I am saying here. Today church means going to a building one or two or three times a week, sitting in a pew, singing songs, listening to a singer, hearing a preacher. After that, you go home, take off your Sunday-go-to-meeting clothes, have a big meal, and take a nap. It is awfully hard for anyone to walk into that mind-set and successfully explain to a person that the ecclesia is an eighteen-hour-a-day, seven-day-a-week . . . community, colony, fellowship, civilization, *a way of life* . . . with Jesus Christ central in all things.

Nonetheless, *you do* need to be within the body of Christ as you set out on an adventure to know Jesus Christ personally and intimately. Your walk with Christ is not supposed to be a solo endeavor. It is supposed to be corporate, involving all believers . . . together. I may be speaking outside the experience and information of most Christians, but that does not change either the fact or the need.

Most American Christians simply do not know much about the depths of Jesus Christ. And practical help in getting to know him is as scarce as chicken molars. Most of us know virtually nothing about a community of believers who corporately pursue knowing and experiencing Jesus Christ personally and intimately, daily!

Now, having said all that, I will tell you that in the next few pages you are going to be given practical help on how to fellowship with Jesus Christ. In fact, what follows is more than how to get to know Jesus Christ intimately; you are about to be given practical help to assist you in *entering into* the Father's fellowship with the Son and the Son's fellowship with the Father.

I only wish that this could happen to you within the experiential life of the ecclesia.

For one thing, each of us needs the ecclesia desperately! Why? Well, for one thing, most of us are not really very disciplined. Few of us have the stick-to-it-iveness that is needed to pursue Christ continuously.

And *that,* dear reader, is *one* reason God gave us the ecclesia! Our pursuit of Christ is supposed to be *corporate.* A *corporate* pursuit of Jesus Christ is what makes us otherwise lone individuals one hundred times stronger in our pursuit of Christ. Pursuing Christ *together* is the *only* way God ever intended for us to pursue him. There is no comparison between the individual pursuit of Christ and the corporate pursuit of Christ. Almost none of us can "make it" individually; almost all of us *can* make it when it is a *corporate* endeavor! That is wonderful news, especially to those of us who are undisciplined! That is also one of the main advantages believers back in the first century had over us.

The Christian life has never worked, does not work, and will never work except within the walls of the city of God. Pursuing Christ in a corporate body of believers—that is God's way. It works even for a peasant like me!

In the meantime, we are stuck with the present situation. Therefore, I close this chapter with a strong recommendation. Find someone interested in knowing the Lord and, obviously, someone who is also reading this book. Find someone willing to give up that entire list of things to do! Find someone willing to abandon the way he prays and start all over from square one! The two of you then get together. Together, pursue the practical matters presented in this book on how to establish an intimate, personal experience with Jesus Christ.

Finally, it is my hope that you will give this venture a great deal of time and that you will carefully follow the practical help presented herein.

PART II

Nowhere will you find
a more untroubled place of
retreat
than in your spirit.

SIXTEEN

Do You Have Four Months?

I once read the story of a man who wanted to pass on some secrets he had learned in his profession. Despite his desire to make this knowledge known, he did not want these secrets to fall into the hands of just anyone, but rather to those who would diligently, single-mindedly pursue them. Therefore, when he came to write down all he knew, he wrote in words so brief that only those who would give everything to the quest would be able to discover what he was revealing. As I sit here today penning these particular pages, I feel a strong identity with that man. And for the same reason, I have chosen to write the following pages in the briefest possible words. The practical helps are there, but they will assist only that reader who gives his or her full attention to what is presented.

The practical helps given herein are offered in the hope that they will be pursued by believers diligent enough and hungry enough to take time to be thorough. These helps are for the hungry-hearted alone. Therefore, because they are presented in such brevity, I would recommend you read over each assignment several times.

You will find a total of four assignments. Everything you need is here, but follow the road map closely. Most who read books of this genre want to simply read the book and hope that something just *happens* to their spiritual life. But transformation by means of someone pouring all you need into you through a hole in the top of your head is not a viable hope!

These assignments require four months of your time. Four months! Yet if you follow what is given here, you just may emerge with a whole new relationship with Jesus Christ.

May I ask that you *not* read Assignment Two until you have finished Assignment One! *This is extremely important!*

Taking four months to do these assignments will move you beyond your present prayer life. You will not move beyond prayer, but simply beyond that which is commonly *perceived* as prayer.

Found herein is nothing more than a way to fellowship with the Father and the Son. *That* is the first thing all of us should be shown as new Christians. The centrality of the secret to the Christian life rests in the relationship of the Father to the Son and the

Son to the Father, and you are now being invited, not by me but by the living God, to come and take a *beginning* step of entering into that incredible relationship.

And when your four months are completed, I would love to hear from you.

SEVENTEEN

Eternal Elements

The following pages contain practical help that should prove to be foundational to your walk with your Lord. These simple assignments could, in fact, be a wonderful foundation in the lives of all Christians.

What you are about to read is *not* presented to you as *the only way* to enter into a meaningful fellowship with your Lord. It is simply *a way*. But we all need somewhere to begin, a starting point, do we not? Such practice, when repeated over a period of months, tends to become organically established in our lives. Repeated practice eventually finds an organic expression that, in time, will become second nature to you.

The purpose of the four assignments laid out in the

next few pages is to help you establish a relationship with your Lord that will, in the unfolding years, take its own unique direction within your life. That is, what is found in this book should eventually fade, and in its place should arise a hallmark of fellowship with Christ that is unique to you alone.

Remember, this book is but an *introduction* to the deeper Christian life. Nonetheless, there *is* an eternal element to be found here. These practical helps are not something to aid you in prayer, but to aid you in establishing an experiential fellowship with your Lord . . . and ultimately these practical matters may aid you in an experiential touch of *oneness* with him.

Please recall what we saw in the early part of this book. We found out what goes on within the Godhead. Any beginning relationship you may have with your Lord *must* contain those same elements found in the fellowship of the Father and the Son. Those elements? Receiving his life so you may live by that life; being loved by him and loving him; hearing him . . . and most of all . . . beholding him. All these elements combine to make up something called *fellowship*. *These* elements are *eternal* and are the bedrock of an experiential Christian walk . . . for all of us. No matter who you are, or on what plane your spiritual life operates, these are constants—immovable constants.

Where do *you* begin? First acknowledge that you *have* received his life in you. Confess your desire to lay hold of that life of his in you, in a vital, living way. Acknowledge that this life, *his* life, is the only life force in the universe that can live the Christian life, and that you are abandoning *your* effort to live the Christian life. Then learn to love and to be loved by him. Quietly, alone, before him . . . love and be loved by him.

You will find in the following pages *one* practical way to make these elements real in your own life and in your fellowship with your Lord. Pursue them. By the end of the four months, you will have moved off that mountain where *you* are central and will have moved to that mountain where Christ is central. In the process there may come, for one instant, a touch of him as he really is, the All in All (1 Cor. 15).

> Gather yourself together
> at least once a day,
> morning or evening.
> —Thomas à Kempis

EIGHTEEN

Assignment One

Your mind wanders. You feel a sense of guilt when you come before your Lord. You also get sleepy. You do not know what to talk to the Lord about. You get distracted. These are the present hindrances that you face in your prayer life.

Is there a solution to all these hindrances? Yes. Definitely, yes.

There are only two things that exist in our realm that belong to and are native to the other realm. One is the Scripture, which is God-breathed. The other is your spirit. Your spirit *belongs* to and is now part of the other realm—that is, it belongs to the spiritual realm. Join these two elements together (your spirit and the God-breathed Scripture, both of which have their roots in that realm that is native to the Father and the Son), and you have a key for opening the realm of things spiritual and for dealing with these age-old hindrances.

First of all, find another believer (preferably someone of your own gender, or perhaps your husband or wife) who has read this book or who will read this book—someone who will get together with you two or three times a week for three or four months. Someone *hungry* to know Christ, someone ready to lay down religiousness! Choose someone who, like you, is willing to lay down religious vocabulary, the pretentious voice tone, even speaking in tongues, and lofty, artful words of praise. Yes, someone *that* hungry.

Second, make a list of three passages of Scripture (in the Old Testament or the New Testament) that are very Christ-centered. The passages need not be over five to eight verses long. These may or may not be your favorite passages. Be careful in your choices. Choose only passages that are very Christological (as in Ephesians and Colossians).

You are about to enter into an ancient and greatly revered practice of the saints of all the centuries past, a practice and a heritage that has been passed down through two millennia of the Christian faith. You are about to turn Scripture into prayer.*

Approaching the Lord by this means, your mind will not wander. You will not get distracted. You will not get sleepy. And you will know *what* to pray. And what you pray will be higher and richer than what

---

* *Praying the Scripture,* by Judson Cornwall. Psalm 23 will be your beginning point; you will *begin* each of your four assignments with Psalm 23. If you have carefully chosen your other three passages of Scripture, you will later be able to use those passages in the same way you use Psalm 23.

you have usually prayed in the past. Why? Because you will be praying the Scripture!

Here is how you begin.

This beginning—before you even open the Scripture—is the most important *practical* part of this book. This is the part that will demand your greatest attention and your best time. Give yourself *time* here, above all else.

Get alone. Get quiet. Calm your mind. Take your time in doing this. Do not pray. Sit before your Lord. Begin to learn to *behold*, not pray! Five minutes . . . ten minutes. Be loved. Love. Yes, love him.

Next, open your Bible to Psalm 23. Speak out loud, *not* silently. *Talk* Psalm 23 to your Lord.

Paraphrase. Or adapt. Let your heart lead; don't stay just with the verse if your heart becomes filled with other sights of him. Let these, too, flow out of your heart and find spoken expression. And above all, when you speak to your Lord, talk to him in shirt-sleeve English! Give up your King James English and prosaic terms.

If some thought jumps out of your spirit—turn that thought into words. Speak this delightful thought to your Lord, out loud.

Note what is happening. You are talking to the Lord Jesus, but you are using Scripture to furnish you with the words to say. Wonder of wonders, you are praying and reading your Bible!

Now let's take a look at just how this prayer might go.

> Lord Jesus, you are my Shepherd. You take care of me. You always have taken care of

me. You are taking care of me now. You will take care of me in the future. I am a lamb. I was made for a shepherd. You are that Shepherd. And it is true, I have never wanted, and right now I have no needs.

Continue your prayer in this way all through Psalm 23. Try to do all of Psalm 23 each morning for a minimum of three mornings a week. Alone. Quietly.

When your first week is up, look at the other passages you are going to be using. See if they "fit," if they can be used in the same way. You may discover that you need to choose some other passages more suited to this kind of prayer. Or it may be that you will need to reword the passage of Scripture you selected, altering the words just a little to make them appropriate for offering them to the Lord as prayer.

After you have spent three mornings alone with Psalm 23 during your first week . . . *then* ask your Christian friend to join you the second week. When you meet, use Psalm 23 the first time. After that, select one of the other passages you have chosen and use it for the second week. During the second week bring this passage to your Lord alone first. Later in the week meet with your friend and offer up this second passage together.

When the two of you meet, sit together quietly for a good long while before doing anything else. And remember, no *religious* praying! When you come to the point that you begin to pray the Scriptures together, talk to your Lord in plain English! Not flowery or King James-ish. (I recommend, to avoid religious language, that you *not use* the King James

Bible.) Do not try to impress one another with your prayers. Be learners, not teachers. Relax!

How, exactly, do two people pray the Scriptures together? Before you start, decide who is taking the odd-numbered verses and who the even-numbered verses. One of you take verse one and turn it into spoken prayer. The other takes verse two, turning it into spoken prayer, etc. But each of you should not hesitate to interrupt or add to the prayer the other one has just prayed. In fact, do exactly that *whenever* something is sparked within your own spirit. Sometimes, then, you may both end up praying something out of each other's verse.

The third week you should meet two or three times alone to talk to your Lord, using one of the passages of Scripture you have chosen. Repeat your assignment of the first week but using this new passage. Speak out loud. Then meet with your partner and pray through that selected passage (preferably at the end of the week). Together, lift that passage in prayer to your Lord.

At the end, sit quietly before your Lord and love him deeply in your spirit.

The fourth week use the next Christological passage of Scripture you have selected. Do the same as you have with the other passages in the past three weeks.

During the fourth week of your first month, and *not before,* read Assignment Two. Assignment Two will surprise you. You must not know what Assignment Two is during those first three weeks of Assignment One.

If you turn the page and read Assignment Two

right now, it may kill the whole adventure before it begins. It is really important that you *not* know what is in Assignment Two before you launch into Assignment One.

Assignment One will aid you greatly in learning how to recognize your spirit, to sit before your Lord, and to love him. These are indispensable. But if you read Assignment Two now, it will affect your ability to do so. Please turn now to the addenda (page 129) and read them. Then go look for a partner who will stick with you for four months. But do not read Assignment Two until the fourth week of this spiritual adventure.

NINETEEN

Assignment Two

Please! Do not read Assignment Two until Assignment One is completed!

Assignment Two is very similar to Assignment One. And Assignment One was strategically important to you because it aided you in learning *how* to turn Scripture into prayer. There is one major difference, and that one difference makes all the difference in the world. The difference is revolutionary. The difference lies in how you approach your Lord. But before we discuss that difference, please make this observation.

Throughout the first month (throughout Assignment One), *you* were the entire center of everything that was prayed. To illustrate:

Lord, you are *my* Shepherd. *I* shall not
want. You make *me* lie down in green
pastures. You restore *my* soul. *My* cup
runneth over. Goodness shall follow *me* all
the days of *my* life.

This is pretty typical of the vantage point of most
of our praying, is it not?

In Assignment Two, you are about to go to a new
mountain, one you might never have been on before.
You are about to look at the Christian faith from a
new vantage point. This time you will totally shift the
center. *You* will no longer be the focal point of the
prayer. And may that simple shift forever change
your life, change the way you view the Christian life,
and even change the way you pray and the way you
use Scripture to pray.

Please consider again. You will never have a *spiritual experience* but what that experience was *first*
known and experienced by Jesus Christ. That is true
of you and of all believers. And it was true of a
shepherd boy named David who wrote Psalm 23.

If this is true, then Psalm 23 was not first experienced by David nor by you. It was *first* experienced
by Jesus Christ. Impossible? Not at all. The Son of
God is free of space-time. He existed before any
human being. You only experience what he first experienced. Remember, too, that your Lord lived in
eternity *before* he lived in time, and he is Lord of
time. Psalm 23 is, if it is nothing else, a chronicle of
experience that took place between the Father and
the Son.

This second month you are going to begin with the

same passage of Scripture (Psalm 23), but with *one very great* difference.

You are going to step completely out of the prayer! Not once while speaking to the Lord will you make a personal reference to yourself. This second month you will be *watching* the fellowship of the Father and the Son. That is, you will be beholding! But you *begin* by loving and being loved. (Please reread Assignment One about waiting before the Lord before you begin.) You will become an *observer* of that eternal exchange of spiritual experience between the Father and the Son. You will actually become an observer (a beholder) of *their* relationship to one another.

Your prayer from Psalm 23, therefore, might come forth something like this:

> Father, when Jesus Christ was here on this earth, you were his Shepherd. He never had any needs. You met all his needs. *You are all* that Jesus Christ has ever needed.

> Lord Jesus, while you lived here on earth, your Father was your rest. You rested in him. He replenished your soul. Your Father was your drink. He was your food. He was your full supply.

> Father, you are the righteousness of Jesus Christ. You are his path. The Lord Jesus moved and lived in your righteousness. He followed you, and he glorified your name.

Notice that you are not part of the prayer. *You just changed mountains!*

Continue offering up Psalm 23 in this way. Stay out

of the prayer. Observe the interchange, the experience, the fellowship that goes on between Father and Son.

Remember, do not begin this prayer immediately. First spend some time waiting quietly before the Lord.

Go through this assignment two or three times the first week, alone. Then meet with your friend *once* at the end of the week. One of you take the even-numbered verses, one of you take the odd-numbered verses. Offer up Psalm 23 together.

The second week, take one of the other passages you have chosen. Continue praying in this manner each remaining week for the entire month.

During the last few days of the second month, read Assignment Three.

Wouldn't this be easier, and wouldn't it be wonderful, if about fifty or a hundred people in the ecclesia were all doing this during the same season and sharing their individual experience with one another in the informality of living rooms scattered throughout your town? With *no* leaders present!

TWENTY

Assignments Three and Four

There are two parts of Assignment Three. The first part: Do nothing but listen. Here's how:

Get alone. Simply sit before your Lord quietly. Love. Be loved. (See Assignment One.) Now open Psalm 23. Do not speak. *Listen!* Listen to the Son speak, but *not* to you. Listen to him speak to the Father. Listen to the Father speak, not to you, but to the Son.

What you hear from Psalm 23 will probably be something like this:

> Father, while I was on earth, I testified
> before men and angels that you shepherded
> me. I witnessed to men and angels that I

never had any need. And that you were always with me.

My Son, while you were on earth I led you. You followed me and glorified my name. I was your drink, I was your rest, and even now, here in the eternals, I am your drink and your rest.

Continue "listening" alone with Psalm 23, two or three times during the first week. This part of the assignment is to be done alone, not with a friend; but your friend should be keeping up with you, following Assignment Three in the same manner. At the end of the week, the two of you meet together and share with one another what you "saw and heard."

This is simply a beholding and listening assignment.

Listening. Beholding.

Do not become part of what you hear; simply listen. Do this with Psalm 23. The second week move to the next passage you have selected. Spend a lot of time listening to the Father and Son speaking to one another. During this second week meet with your partner again at the end of the week and share with one another what you have heard as you *listened* to Father and Son fellowshiping together. Just share, nothing more!

Repeat this the third and fourth weeks, using new passages each week. Linger in your beholding and listening.

The *second* part of Assignment Three is very simple. That is, at the beginning of Assignment Three, write and ask for Assignment Four. This fourth assignment is only for those who have passed through Assignments One, Two, and Three!*

When you receive your fourth assignment, along with it you will also receive some other simple observations and help for the weeks that lie ahead. *Do not* write until you have done Assignments One and Two and have *begun* Assignment Three. No cheating!

And Assignment Four will be the *beginning!*

May you find his riches and him who is richness.

And what will you have gained in all this when your fourth month is up?

You will have joined into the fellowship of the Godhead. (So will a friend of yours!) You will have learned a little bit more about your spirit—the sense of your spirit and its location in you. You will be learning to differentiate between your spirit and your emotions and will. You will have learned to love, to behold, to listen, to respond . . . *to fellowship with him.* And, hopefully, you will have learned (on some of these occasions) to absent yourself and simply behold the Godhead in fellowship.

And that should be your introduction to the deeper Christian life.

SeedSowers

Christian Books Publishing House

P.O Box 3317
Jacksonville, FL. 32206
800-228-2665

www.seedsowers.com

* Write to: Gene Edwards, .

ADDENDA

*Any time Christians do
anything
three times in a row...
it becomes a New Testament
doctrine!*

Observations and Warnings

I would like for you to return with me to a classroom at Southwestern Baptist Theological Seminary, back when I was a young minister in that seminary.

The class had about forty students in it. Most of us were in our last year in seminary. Our professor posed a question to the class.

"What is the main thing, the central issue, for which Baptists stand?"

There was a moment's pause, then hands began to go up. One young seminarian said, "The main thing Baptists stand for is water baptism . . . baptism by immersion."

The professor answered, "No, that is not correct."

Another student was recognized, and his response

was, "The central thing Baptists stand for is *once saved, always saved* . . . the security of the believer."

Our professor slowly, deliberately shook his head.

Another hand went up. "We stand for the Bible as being the infallible Word of God."

There was a long pause. We looked at the student; we looked at our professor. Again, a negative. At that point the room fell silent.

Every man in that classroom was a college graduate. All of us were near the end of our seminary training. I was twenty-two years old at the time and was ending almost four years of seminary study. I had studied Greek and Hebrew. I had been a voracious reader of the Bible and one of the most frequent shelf browsers ever to wander that seminary's library. But that morning I joined thirty-nine other students who did not have the foggiest idea what Baptists mainly stood for.

After what seemed to be a very, very long time, our professor gave the answer. The centrality of all that Baptists stand for is Jesus Christ.

That was the first and only time in all of my theological education that I had ever heard that statement made. Of course, everyone in the room was embarrassed. But to me the question is, why were forty seminary students so unutterably dumb? Had that same question been asked in any classroom in any Protestant seminary in the world, probably the same thing would have happened. Rarely is the Lord Jesus Christ ever revealed to us . . . *gloriously* revealed. And rarely, if ever, is Jesus Christ revealed to be our *centrality* (I mean revealed so as to become *revelation).* Depending on the Bible as our centrality is easier to do because we do not have to face experiential reality. To tell people Christ is central implies there is a way he can be *made* central . . . experientially.

I would like to pursue this point with you a bit further, but before doing so, I would like to tell you another story. Perhaps you have heard it, but it bears repeating.

It is a story about the famous Chinese Christian named Watchman Nee. The story illuminates our lack of insight for seeing Christ as central in our lives.

I hold in my heart the cherished memory of the lady who first told me this story. She was an elderly, very saintly woman named Beta Shyrick. Beta had been a Methodist missionary in China. She eventually left that mission and became a co-worker to Watchman Nee. The story she told me had to do with Nee's mentor, a woman who was called Sister Barber. It is one of those stories I will never forget because it was told to me by someone actually involved.

As a young man in his early twenties, Nee was under the tutorship of Sister Barber. One day young Nee came to Miss Barber with a very thick dissertation he had written on eschatology. It was a premillennial discussion of the signs and symbols found in Daniel, Ezekiel, and Revelation. Sister Barber said to young Nee, "You do not wish to take this direction in your ministry." Her simple statement arrested Nee and his enthusiasm for speculation about the second coming of Christ.

On yet another day, this exuberant young Chinese burst into Sister Barber's house and told her that he had just heard one of the best speakers he had ever listened to. "Here is a really great Christian who knows the Lord," said Nee. Sister Barber went with Nee to a meeting and heard the man speak. After the meeting was over she gave the following observation: "This man has a great deal of power, but internally he knows very, very little of the Lord Jesus Christ." Nee was stunned.

Sometime later, Nee came to Sister Barber's house again, full of enthusiasm. "You must hear a man I have just heard. He is filled with the Lord. This time you will really be impressed." Sister Barber once more went with Nee to hear a visiting minister who was speaking to Christians in that city. After hearing the man speak, Sister Barber had this to say.

"This is a highly intelligent man. He has a brilliant understanding of the Scripture. He is a very eloquent speaker. But internally he knows very little of the Lord Jesus Christ." Again, Nee was astounded.

Sometime later, Nee once more burst into Sister Barber's home. "I found a man who really knows the Lord. Everything that he says lets you know that this man walks with the Lord Jesus. You must come hear this godly man. I am sure this time you will agree with me."

Once more Sister Barber went with young Watchman Nee to hear a speaker. This time her observations were slightly different. Listen very carefully to her words.

"Many years ago this man had a profound experience with Jesus Christ. It was an experience that changed his life and brought brokenness into his life; but he has been living on that experience and preaching on that experience ever since. He does not have an up-to-date, *present* walk with the Lord. He is operating on a past encounter with God."

On this occasion something got through to Nee. You might say that Nee began to realize what few Christians realize. He began to see the necessity of the importance of having a living, up-to-date, *experiential* relationship with Jesus Christ. All doctrine, all teaching, all power, all practice, all concepts, all creeds pale into insignificance and bow to one point: the centrality of Jesus Christ in all things.

Your Lord is to be experienced.

During the years I have been conducting conferences on the deeper Christian life (and other conferences on experiencing Jesus Christ *within the body of Christ*), I have often thought back to this story. If Sister Barber, though she long ago went to be with the Lord, were sitting in a meeting where I was speaking, what would she say? While I am speaking, do the words I speak and the message I bring indicate a present, up-to-date, experiential, daily, intimate encounter with my Lord?

Well, dear reader, let me react to that thought. First of all, this writer will never attain the status of "holy man." I was raised by a Cajun father in an oil field environment. As far as the eye could see, we were all roughnecks. (That's ten strikes against a fellow right there!) I have an awful lot of rough edges that reflect my growing up in a poor, uneducated family of rough-and-tumble oil field people . . . in east Texas of all places! I just do not look, act, or talk . . . holy! At best, I am roughly shod.

Despite my very rough edges and total inability to

project a "holy" image, there may have been times that Sister Barber would have said of me, "This man is exalting a present, living, reigning, victorious Lord whom he personally, presently knows and experiences. I wish every Christian knew and experienced our Lord in the way he has been presented here." (I may really be presuming too much here. I understand, from all Beta told me, that Sister Barber was one hard lady to impress—and so was Beta!) But there would probably have been times when Sister Barber would have said, and said truthfully, "This man is not speaking from a present, up-to-date experience with Jesus Christ."

One thing I do know today, however, that I did not know back in that seminary class—I now know the answer to my professor's question!

Dear reader, the point of this chapter is simple. Chances are, the centrality of your life is not Jesus Christ. What is? Of course, I do not know the answer to that question. It very well may be *serving* Jesus Christ. Certainly serving Jesus Christ is a big god in the world today. Is that your god? Is it preaching or some other ministry or mission? Or soul saving? Or tongues? Or family? Or security? *You know what it is.* Lay it down!

Drop everything! Pursue knowing him!

But just before you do, you might find it wise to read the next chapter!

The Danger of Knowing Him

Tragedy, persecution, and death have befallen many a believer who has pulled away from the moorings of everyday Christianity. Others more fortunate only got into a lot of *trouble*. This chapter is about that fact. This chapter also serves as a warning to you. By the way, just about all the books ever penned on the subject of getting to know Jesus Christ in the depths (if written before 1900) had a chapter like this!

Let us go back and try to understand why a room full of seminary students did not know the answer to the question posed to us that day at Southwestern. It is a good place to begin understanding how getting to really know your Lord can get you into serious trouble.

Why did these students not know the answer to

that simple question? Unfortunately, the reason is appallingly clear. The Christian family does not talk about the Lord as our centrality because we do not know him on a personal, daily, intimate basis. This is foreign territory.

True, Jesus Christ is preached from the pulpits of churches all over the world every Sunday. Sometimes he is preached as a great comforter. Sometimes he is preached as a battering ram to scare people out of their skin. Sometimes he is presented as a vengeful Lord who has just caught you sinning and who will, if you don't stop sinning, punish the daylights out of you. Sometimes he is preached as a doctrine; and when he is, the minister lets us know we are to be vehemently opposed to those Christians down the street who preach a *different* doctrine. But sometimes the Lord Jesus is preached as Savior; and it is at that point, the point of salvation, that the Lord is presented to us as one who is *experience-able*. Only in the message of salvation, and virtually nowhere else, do we hear of a Lord who can be presently known and experienced. Dumbfounding!

Do not misunderstand me. *Prayer* is preached to us all the time. And we have prayer meetings, do we not? And most of those prayer meetings are so dead, or boring, that they would put a rock to sleep! About the closest we really get to knowing and touching this One who is our centrality is when the congregation stands and sings a beautiful hymn of praise.

Of course, charismatics and Pentecostals have a heyday getting to know the Lord through speaking in tongues. (Most of you charismatic folks will not own up to having worn out tongues years ago or admit that a lot of what you do is pure, unadulterated pretense.) Nonetheless, you who are charismatics and Pentecostals are a mile ahead of the rest of us evangelicals when it comes to touching the Lord. Still, most of what you have to offer is often not much more than an emotional juggernaut. Please do not take this as a criticism; it is simply an observation. Personally, I have encouraged many a dry, dead Baptist to go find some Pentecostal who will pray over him in hopes that perhaps, if he spoke in tongues, he just might rip loose from all of the attachments to dead things that Baptists, and the rest of us evangelicals, are so glued to. Nonetheless, you dear, proud charismatic Pentecostals, so smug and so sure that you have a corner on Jesus Christ, the half has not been fancied *even by you*, as to how rich and how personal the Lord Jesus Christ is, and how intimately he can be known in the daily life of all believers. Come on, Pentecostals, loosen up! Even you might find something higher than and—perish the thought—other than tongues.

Will the day come when seminary students will really know the answer to my professor's question? Are things going to get any better in the area of our hearing about a deeper, more personal, and more intimate walk with Jesus Christ? What is your guess? Here is mine.

You have often heard it said, "The problem with Christians *today* is . . ." or *"Today's* Christians don't . . ." or *"Today's* Christians need . . ." Well, dear reader, I hate to tell you this, but this problem of Christians not knowing their Lord very well is not just today's problem. This problem was around with yesterday's Christians, *and* the day before yesterday's Christians. You can push that back all the way through the last seventeen hundred years. It has been *that* long since Jesus Christ was the intimate, experience-able centrality of the Christian's faith! Somewhere between A.D. 300 and 400, *Christ* got pushed out. Doctrines, teachings, power, prophecy, miracles, methods, church buildings, ritual, intellectualism, and a great deal of beautiful preaching came in to take his place. Things have not been all that great ever since. Will things get better? If you are speaking of a large number of people, the answer is no, not likely.

Ever since Constantine made Christianity the official religion of the Western world, there have been an awful lot of Christians. Maybe too many! But since that time, there have been only a few believers who, above all else, have sought to know the Lord Jesus in a very personal continuing walk. That is the way it was, that is the way it is, and that is the way it is probably going to stay . . . right on up until the trumpet sounds.

If you question this assessment, then consider the following story. It is a pretty undeniable indication that most Christians are not really focused on getting to know their Lord better.

On many occasions I have stood before large groups of ministers and spoken of the need of knowing Jesus Christ intimately, and of *this* being the central issue in the believer's life. In fact, I have preached at conventions where preachers were ten feet deep and a mile wide—wall-to-wall preachers! In such messages I have sometimes made the following

statement: It is possible to know Jesus Christ personally, intimately, and daily. Furthermore, it is also
possible to step outside of space-time, outside of this
realm into the other realm, and there personally
know and encounter your Lord, to worship him and
fellowship with him *there,* in another realm.

Now dear reader, give me this: That is one very
heavy statement. That statement begs to be chal-
lenged, accepted, or at least inquired of! For the last
twenty-five years I have sought to declare but one
thing, the Lord Jesus Christ. I hope he has been the
central theme of my ministry for all these years. And
often, when speaking of him at conferences, I have
been "Amen-ed," I have been applauded, I have been
cheered, and, yes, I have even had standing ovations.
Yet, in all those twenty-five years, not once has any
minister of the gospel ever walked up to me and said,
"Gene, show me how to personally, intimately experience my Lord every day." And not one minister of the
gospel has ever said to me, "Show me how to step
outside of space-time into that other realm and fellowship with my Lord there."

Only once did a layman do so! One lone soul in
twenty-five years!

From this I draw a conclusion. (It took me twenty-
five years to reach this conclusion!) My conclusion is
that Christians love to be preached to, love to be
swept over by the power of preaching, love to be
thrilled and chilled, love to exult in what has been
said, and love to go to conferences where all these
wonderful things happen . . . but they have heard so
many glorious sermons that have given so little practical help that they have reached a point where they

do not really believe that intimately knowing Jesus Christ can be made practical. They have subconsciously concluded that knowing him cannot be laid hold of in concrete terms.

Back to the original point. Do not expect, either yesterday or today or tomorrow, to discover a lot of interest among Christians in getting to know the Lord intimately. That is just the way things are and the way things have been. And unless something radically new emerges on the pages of history, this is the way things will remain, as history itself will attest.

Be clear on this matter, dear reader: The reason we have not been given help in this area is that the generation before us did not receive practical help. And the reason that generation did not help them is because they did not receive any help from their fathers, etc. This is a seventeen-hundred-year-old story!

Based on empirical observation of forty years in the ministry and forty-two years as a Christian, with the exception of a few voraciously hungry and desperately thirsty believers who really believe that Jesus Christ is all there is to the Christian faith, this is simply the unchanging status quo. I have asked a number of other ministers who have been in the ministry as long as I have and who have spoken to far more people in far more places than I have. Their concern is much the same as mine.

Nonetheless, he can be known, more intimately than you have ever dreamed. Are *you* one of the desperate?

Which brings us to a simple question: Just *how*

desperate are you to know him? Enough to lay down all those things that have missed the main point—all those things that have put the main point back there at the back of the room? Enough to lay down that weird way you pray? (You think you don't pray in a weird way? Tape one of your spoken prayers and listen to it!) Will you make an intimate fellowship with the Godhead, which is the wellspring of the Christian life, your primary pursuit? Can you lay down your pet doctrines, and the Lord knows what else, to *know* him?

If you can lay down all other things, it still will not be easy to rid yourself of them and walk away from them. If it is easy for you to do so, you did not lay them down! Or you laid down the wrong things!

Now here comes the hard part. Keep in mind that the experience of knowing Jesus Christ is *supposed* to take place within the informal fellowship of the body of Christ. To know your Lord within this wonderful place sometimes called (1) the colony of the believers, (2) a colony from heaven, (3) the ecclesia, (4) church life, etc. . . . to know him *there* is a present need in your life and mine.*

You do not live in a day in which the deep things of Christ are fervently pursued, nor do you live in a day when the church is a community of the believers. You probably will not get a great deal of encouragement from Christians to make either of these your life's

---

* "Going to church" may not stir this author a great deal. But the church, the ecclesia, has been the passion of my life and the experience of my life. I am *for* the church. I am so much for the church that I don't take to her being made a one-hour-per-week gathering. The church is supposed to be our very matrix!

pursuit . . . especially if you begin laying down *other* things.

Our forefathers have been off chasing *something* . . . something *other than* knowing him . . . for generations. Every generation, it seems, finds a different *something* to chase after. What do we chase today? For sure, something other than him! We live in an era bent on evangelism and soul winning, on activity, on doing, on accomplishments and success. Unbelievably, we live in a day when most of the fun and excitement of being a Christian is not even associated with the word *church*. The church is thought of as a place to go on Sunday. Things such as fun, a great vision, and excitement are found today mostly in the nondenominational movements. The thought of all the local ecclesia being the dynamic spearhead of *all* things that have to do with the Kingdom of God virtually never enters our minds.

Which brings us to *you!* Will you return to the centrality and supremacy of Jesus Christ, daily and experientially . . . *within the ecclesia?* Until God's people make so radical and revolutionary a turn, everything else is on hold because the ecclesia is the only place where the Scripture makes sense and the only place the Christian life works!

All those Scriptures quoted to you as an individual will *never* become workable; they work *only* in the church. (Check those verses. Most were written to churches!) And all those seminars with their charts, graphs, syllabi, etc., will never work because knowing Christ only works for a believer in the context of something called church life.

Your Lord is alive. Dear reader, he dwells within

you. He is the most exciting being in all creation. He can be known far beyond anything most of us have ever conceived. He was meant to be the centrality of all your life! What do you say? Will this become your magnificent obsession?

"But what of others? Should I not try to bring others to such a pursuit?"

You are not responsible for others! You *are* responsible for *yourself.*

Perhaps there will come a day when people are so full of a daily, personal, intimate relationship with Jesus Christ that he will be all that they proclaim. And in that day they will be able to step down from their exalted platforms of oratory and say, "Let's make this work in our daily lives. Let's make knowing Jesus Christ practical . . . and central."

But that will take a revolution. That will *be* a revolution.

Right now, you cannot pin your hopes on such a dream! Nonetheless, will you allow yourself to be one of those who deny all in order to know him? If you do, you need to remember that many people down through the ages have gotten into an awful lot of trouble when Jesus Christ became everything to them. The great historian Will Durant said it best in *The Story of Civilization.*

> For the last sixteen hundred years the church has persecuted two groups of people: those who do not follow the teachings of Jesus Christ, and those who do.

Are you sure you really want to get to know your Lord intimately? You *are* sure?! Then let me rephrase the question. Are you ready to face the possibility of losing all your friends and being ostracized from the fellowship of believers you meet with, ending up being the biggest and worst rumor circulating in town? And if you get in such a mess, can you handle that mess all alone? You need to answer that question, because things often go in just that direction. Don't ask me why this happens. I do not know. It just does.

You have been warned.

ADDENDUM III

Are Only the Literate
Invited to the Fullness of
the Christian Life?*

Matthew could read. John could read. Perhaps one or two others of the followers of Jesus could read. The rest were illiterate. (The Sanhedrin once noted that these rough fishermen could not distinguish one letter of the Hebrew alphabet from another.)

In that day, written literature was found in schools for the rich, in the temple, and in private ownership of books. Only the wealthy could educate their chil-

---

* I trust the reader will note that I have presented the ecclesia as paramount in, and essential to, the Christian life and have presented prayer and the Scriptures as a means to fellowship with the Godhead. (I am for prayer, Bible, and church!) But do not mistake my words in either direction. I am for the church, prayer, and Scripture; but we need a higher expression of church life and of prayer. And we need to back away from a scenario that *seems* to exalt the Bible *over* the centrality of Christ. This section of the addendum is intended, therefore, simply as a presentation of facts that may loosen up those who seem to demand that the Christian life cannot exist apart from literacy.

dren in actual schools. Outside of these schools (and the synagogues), the ability to read (not to mention write) was about as rare as astrophysics is to our society. How many astrophysicists do you know? Consequently, even if people in Jesus' day could read, there were virtually no books available for them to read.

Also during this particular period in Israel's history, the people's language was in transition. Old Hebrew had died out. Even when read in the synagogue, no one understood it. Reading old Hebrew was a tradition, like reading Latin at a graduation ceremony at an ivy league college is today. The language everyone spoke in the street was a dialect called Aramaic. Like any local dialect, it had rarely been reduced to writing. Literature in Aramaic was confined virtually altogether to simple business transactions. The skill of reading and writing was mostly a service you rented and paid for. If you needed to write a letter or draw up a document, you hired a literate person to do it for you—not unlike the way you hire a computer programmer today.

A new Hebrew was just emerging, but literature in this language was only beginning to appear. That left Latin and Greek. But Latin and Greek were languages new to Israel and were the tongues of the foreign occupation troops, the despised heathen. Some people in Israel were learning those two languages, but that again was confined mostly to the wealthy and influential, and to that tiny group that today would be referred to as middle class, the tradesmen and merchants. Ordinary people such as fishermen simply never learned to read or write their own languages. There were no schools for the poor. And the poor made up well over 95 percent of the population! (A few in these ranks did learn to read, usually because their mother had this skill passed down to her by her parents. This type of learning has sometimes been called "the madonna school" and constituted the main source a poor person had of becoming literate. This went on for about two thousand years.) The twelve, like virtually all the people of Galilee and Judea, were from that 95 percent. If any of them could read, their mothers probably taught this skill to them at home.

These are facts. That they are facts we dare not face (lest our whole modern-day concept of how to live the Christian life crumbles) does not make these facts any less true.

Do not impose your present-day understanding of literacy on people living two thousand years ago. In ancient days illiteracy was not a sign of ignorance, *nor* was literacy a sign of intelligence. To a large extent, literacy was a trade, similar to cabinetmaking or carpentry or television repair. (How many television repairmen do you know? Well, in Jesus' day there was about *that* percentage of people who were skilled at reading and writing.) We must not impose what literacy means today upon any society anywhere on earth before A.D. 1700! In other words, the ability to read and write did not become a viable force in the general human society until just three hundred years ago.

Yet, despite these facts, from one end of the English-speaking world to the other, it is heralded from every evangelical pulpit, "You must read your Bible to be a good Christian." That statement might sound like a sensible statement, *after* the year A.D. 1700. But that statement would have made no sense at all to *any* society on earth previous to that time.

In the days of Martin Luther, for instance, when the printed word has been credited with bringing in the Reformation, the maximum number of people who would read what Luther wrote stood at about 5 percent! About 90 percent of that part of Europe affected by the Reformation was totally illiterate. Another 5 percent was only functionally literate. That 5 percent was either too poor to buy Reformation literature or lacked the vocabulary skills to understand the writings of a Luther, a Melanchthon, a Calvin, or a Zwingli. So 5 percent of the population could read Reformation literature. Yet we have been given the impression that *everyone* was in on the Reformation and that study of the Scriptures by the masses brought in the Reformation!

The message that you *must* read your Bible every day to be a good Christian would have been irrelevant to most average Christians even as late as 1800! (At least 85 percent of all the Southern boys who fought in the Civil War, 1860–1865, could *not* read, and of those who could read, most were only semiliterate and did *not* read.) The message "Read your Bible" became relevant to most lower-class people in the English-speaking world only by the mid-1800s and the early 1900s. The same was true for any place else on earth! Before that time, this statement was the equivalent of saying, "You must have a master's degree from the university in order to be a good Christian." A master's degree *now* and the ability to read three hundred years ago had almost the same percentage of people in its ranks.

The twentieth century needs desperately to ask the first century: Did Jesus Christ tie the victorious Christian life to being able to read? If he did, he certainly demonstrated poor judgment in picking his closest followers! We need to face up to this. Did God, faced with a choice between literacy for his followers or indwelling them . . . did he choose literacy? Which opens more doors for more people to know him?

Today three-fifths of the people on our planet are still illiterate! We are, therefore, driven back again and again to this question: If literacy is necessary to the living out of the Christian life, what place have illiterates in knowing Christ?

There *is* a way for the illiterate Christian to be equal to the literate Christian in knowing Christ. He need only be introduced to a few essentials about his salvation, the first of these being that he has an indwelling Lord! He need only learn to locate the place of residence of the Lord who lives in him and begin fellowshiping with that Lord. If the key to living the Christian life is not an indwelling Lord, then whatever else is picked as being that key is drastically limiting the number of people who can enter in. Evangelists of this age are very close to elitism, snobbishness, *and* the allocation of the Christian life to educated people, as they insist that Christians must have an almost total mastery of the contents of the New Testament. To talk to God's people in such a way is to demonstrate a monumental ignorance of history, as well as a blind refusal to look at historical facts.

How many seminary professors and pastors have come from visiting remote villages in Nepal, Africa, and the jungles of Indochina to declare they have just beheld the most beautiful expression of the church they have ever beheld in all their lives, yet without it ever occurring to them that these beautiful Christians were virtually all illiterate! And those seminary professors were right. The most beautiful expression of church life on this earth today is in foreign lands among poor, uneducated, illiterate people! Scholars, seminarians, and other assorted Bible authorities, please take note!

We believers, whose ranks are spread among tribes and nations over this planet, have but one common factor among us: a living, moving, speaking Lord who dwells inside each of us. That indwelling Lord is the only one with the resources to live the Christian life. To point to anything else as the answer to the Christian life cuts off most of us from effectively living the Christian life. Or do we dare believe God confines his best only to people who can read! Try defending that idea anywhere, any time before 1700, and you would be considered some kind of nut! Ditto for those who confine the victorious Christian life to tongues, or a college education, or Bible school attendance.*

Find him who lives inside of you and get to know him. And read the inspired Scriptures daily. But never insist that literacy is essential to an effective Christian life. *Jesus Christ* is the one necessity to living the Christian life.

---

* The conclusion drawn here does not necessarily reflect the views of the vast majority of seminary professors. (I just thought you would like to know that.)

Recommended Reading

Christ Esteem *by Don Matzat*
Classical Christianity *by Bob George*
The Normal Christian Life *by Watchman Nee*
Prayer: Conversing with God *by Rosalind Rinker*
Living by the Highest Life *by Gene Edwards*

Gene Edwards can be contacted at:

Destiny Ministries
P.O. Box 3450
Jacksonville, FL 32206
www.geneedwards.com

SEEDSOWERS
800-228-2665   (fax) 904-598-3456
www.seedsowers.com

REVOLUTIONARY BOOKS ON CHURCH LIFE

How to Meet In Homes (*Edwards*) 10.95
An Open Letter to House Church Leaders (*Edwards*) 4.00
When the Church Was Led Only by Laymen *(Edwards)* 4.00
Beyond Radical (*Edwards*) 5.95
Rethinking Elders (*Edwards*) 9.95
Revolution, The Story of the Early Church (*Edwards*) 8.95
The Silas Diary (*Edwards*) 9.99
The Titus Diary (*Edwards*) 8.99
The Timothy Diary (*Edwards*) 9.99
The Priscilla Diary (*Edwards*) 9.99
The Gaius Diary *(Edwards)* 10.99
Overlooked Christianity (*Edwards*) 14.95
Pagan Christianity *(Viola)* 13.95

AN INTRODUCTION TO THE DEEPER CHRISTIAN LIFE

Living by the Highest Life (*Edwards*) 10.99
The Secret to the Christian Life (*Edwards*) 8.99
The Inward Journey (*Edwards*) 8.99

CLASSICS ON THE DEEPER CHRISTIAN LIFE

Experiencing the Depths of Jesus Christ (*Guyon*) 8.95
Practicing His Presence (*Lawrence/Laubach*) 8.95
The Spiritual Guide (*Molinos*) 8.95
Union With God (*Guyon*) 8.95
The Seeking Heart (*Fenelon*) 9.95
Intimacy with Christ (*Guyon*) 10.95
The Song of the Bride *(Guyon)* 9.95
Spiritual Torrents (*Guyon*) 10.95
The Ultimate Intention (*Fromke*) 11.00
One Hundred Days in the Secret Place *(Edwards)* 12.99

IN A CLASS BY ITSELF

The Divine Romance (*Edwards*) 8.95

NEW TESTAMENT

The Story of My Life as Told by Jesus Christ *(Four gospels blended)* 14.95
Acts in First Person *(Book of Acts)* 9.95

COMMENTARIES BY JEANNE GUYON

Genesis Commentary 10.95
Exodus Commentary 10.95
Leviticus - Numbers - Deuteronomy Commentaries 12.95
Judges Commentary 7.95
Job Commentary 10.95
Song of Songs *(Song of Solomon Commentary)* 9.95
Jeremiah Commentary 7.95
James - I John - Revelation Commentaries 12.95

THE CHRONICLES OF HEAVEN *(Edwards)*

THE COLLECTED WORKS OF T. AUSTIN-SPARKS

COMFORT AND HEALING

OTHER BOOKS ON CHURCH LIFE

CHRISTIAN LIVING

Prices subject to change

The Chronicles of Heaven

by

Gene Edwards

The Old Testament

The Beginning covers *Genesis*, chapters 1&2 (*The Promise* will come next, covering the rest of *Genesis*). *The Escape*, already in print, covers *Exodus*. Other volumes will follow until the Pentateuch is finished.

In *The Beginning* God creates the heavens and the earth. The crowning glory of creation is man and woman, who live and move in both the visible world and the spiritual world.

Experience one of the greatest events of human history: *The Escape* of the Israelite people from Egypt. Watch the drama from that of earthly participants and that of the angels in the heavens.

Experience the wonderful story of the incarnation, the Christmas story, seen from both realms. *The Birth* introduces the mystery of the Christian life for those who have never heard the story.

The New Testament

The Chronicles then extend into the *New Testament*. They are *The Birth* and *The Triumph*. After *The Triumph* comes *The First–Century Diaries* !

In *The Triumph* you will experience the Easter story as you never have before. Join angels as they comprehend the suffering and death of Jesus and the mystery of free will in light of God's Eternal Purpose.

The Door. It has moved to a hill on Patmos. What would John be allowed to see? Come along and witness the finale of the stirring conclusion to *The Chronicles of Heaven.*

AN INTRODUCTION TO
THE DEEPER CHRISTIAN LIFE

In Three Volumes
by
Gene Edwards

1. Living by the Highest Life

If you find yourself unsettled with Christianity as usual ... If you find yourself longing for a deeper experience of the Christian life ... *The Highest Life* is for you.

Did Jesus Christ live the Christian life merely by human effort? Or did Jesus understand living by the Spirit—His Father's life in Him?

Discover what it means to live a spiritual life while living on earth.

2. Secret to the Christian Life

Read the Bible, pray, go to church, tithe ... is this what it means to live the Christian life? Is there more to living the Christian life than following a set of rules? How did Jesus live by the Spirit?

The Secret to the Christian Life reveals the one central secret to living out the Christian life. Nor does the book stop there ... it also gives *practical* ways to enhance your fellowship with the Lord.

3. The Inward Journey

The Inward Journey is the companion volume to *The Secret to the Christian Life*. A beautiful story of a dying uncle explaining to his nephew—a new Christian–the ways and mysteries of the cross and of suffering. Of those who have a favorite Gene Edwards book, tens of thousands have selected *The Inward Journey* as that book.

The next book in this series by Gene Edwards is entitled *The Inward Journey* . . . it is about the necessary work of the cross in your life as a believer.